A Vegan Taste of Greece

Other cookbooks by Linda Majzlik published by Jon Carpenter

Party Food for Vegetarians
Vegan Dinner Parties
Vegan Baking
Vegan Barbecues and Buffets
A Vegan Taste of the Caribbean
A Vegan Taste of Italy
A Vegan Taste of India
A Vegan Taste of Mexico
A Vegan Taste of the Middle East
A Vegan Taste of France
A Vegan Taste of North Africa

A Vegan Taste
of Greece

Linda Majzlik

JON CARPENTER

Our books may be ordered from bookshops or (post free) from
Jon Carpenter Publishing, Alder House, Market Street, Charlbury,
England OX7 3PH

Credit card orders may be phoned or faxed to 01689 870437
or 01608 811969

First published in 2003 by
Jon Carpenter Publishing
Alder House, Market Street, Charlbury, Oxfordshire OX7 3PH
☎ 01608 811969

© Linda Majzlik 2003

Illustrations by Amanda Henriques © 2003

The right of Linda Majzlik to be identified as author of this work has been
asserted in accordance with the Copyright, Design and Patents Act 1988

ISBN 1 897766 84 X

Printed in England by J. W. Arrowsmith Ltd., Bristol

CONTENTS

Baking

INTRODUCTION

Greece occupies the southern section of the Balkan peninsula and consists of the mainland, bordering Albania, Macedonia, Bulgaria and Turkey, and more than 2,000 islands, many of which are uninhabited. The islands are spread over a vast area, from the Ionian Sea in the west to the Aegean Sea in the east, and together they make up about one fifth of the total land mass. The south of Greece enjoys a subtropical Mediterranean climate, while northern parts are cooler and have distinct seasons. As nearly three-quarters of the country is mountainous, much of the land is unsuitable for growing crops, but the central plains of Thessaly and the northern plains of Thrace and Macedonia have fertile soils. The main crops grown in these areas are barley, wheat, corn and sugar beet, and southern parts of the mainland and the islands are famous for their grapes, tomatoes, olives and citrus fruits.

Throughout their long history the Greeks have invaded and have been invaded by many other peoples. The legacy of these past invasions lives on in the variety of cooking styles throughout the country. In the southern areas Mediterranean flavours predominate, while in the northern and central areas more spicy foods are enjoyed, serving as a reminder of the invaders from the East. As in many other Southern European countries, traditional Greek cuisine relies mainly on seasonal produce and preserving these foods by pickling, bottling and drying is done in many homes.

Family life lies at the heart of Greek society and it is not unusual for several generations of the same family to live under one roof, especially in rural areas. As well as living together families tend to socialise together and eating out in the many local restaurants, tavernas and cafés is a favourite pastime. Even the smallest village has a café which serves coffee, alcohol and soft drinks as well as cakes and snacks. They are usually open long hours and act as a lively social hub for the village. It is often said that no part of Greece is more than 85 miles from the sea and picnics on the beach are also very popular. Many of the mezedes can be easily transported and together with salads, breads, desserts and cakes they make ideal picnic foods.

The majority of the population is Greek Orthodox and the calendar is dominated by religious festivals, feast days, saints' days and holidays. Religious celebrations are deeply rooted in Greek culture and special foods are traditionally prepared for these occasions. Examples are Lenten cake, Easter biscuits, Christmas bread, St. Basil's bread and halva, which is a traditional Lenten sweet.

As well as the numerous religious festivals, hardly a week goes by without other festivities, such as name days, carnivals, national holidays and cultural festivals, many off which involve great family get-togethers, dancing and the sharing of a bounteous spread.

Easter is by far the most important and sacred festival of the year and it is preceded by the 40 days of Lent, during time which no meat, eggs or dairy products are eaten. Greeks also do not eat these foods on Wednesdays and Fridays throughout the year. As a result there is a whole range of dishes completely free of animal products and so eminently suitable for vegans.

THE VEGAN GREEK STORECUPBOARD

Traditional Greek cuisine is based around fresh seasonal produce and meals are prepared according to what is in season. Other ingredients with a longer shelf life are regularly used and the following will help create some authentic-tasting dishes.

Almonds Rich in protein, B vitamins, vitamin E and calcium, almonds are used in numerous sweet recipes and occasionally in savoury dishes. Their flavour is enhanced if lightly toasted.

Artichoke hearts As fresh artichokes are only seasonally available, tinned or bottled artichoke hearts have been used for convenience. These simply need to be rinsed before use.

Barley Believed to be the first cultivated grain, barley is one of the main crops grown in Greece. Pearl barley has been stripped of important nutrients in the milling process, so whole or pot barley is more nutritious. Barley is an ingredient in various dishes, as well as simply being served cooked with casseroles and stews.

Beans Although tinned beans are a useful standby, it is worth cooking dried beans in bulk as they freeze successfully. All beans are a good source of protein, fibre and minerals and popular varieties in Greece are haricot, flageolet, cannellini and butter.

Breadcrumbs No bread is wasted in Greece so stale bread is often made into crumbs and used in various savoury recipes. Crumbs can easily be made by whizzing bread in a food processor or nut mill. They can be stored in the freezer and used from frozen.

Bulgar wheat Made from dried, crushed wheat berries which have had the bran removed, bulgar simply needs to be soaked in liquid. It is a versatile grain and is regularly used as a stuffing for vegetables or mixed with other ingredients in salads. Bulgar wheat can also be added to casserole dishes or served on its own or mixed with other grains as an accompaniment.

Capers The small green flower buds from a trailing bush, capers have a piquant taste and are sold preserved in either vinegar or brine. They are used as an ingredient and as a garnish.

'Cheese' Used regularly both as an ingredient or simply as a garnish. White cheddar-style substitutes made from soya are a good alternative to feta.

Chickpeas These creamy, nutty-flavoured peas combine well with all other ingredients and are commonly used in dips, soups, casseroles and salads. They are highly nutritious and a good source of protein, fibre, vitamins and minerals.

Cornflour A very fine starchy white flour milled from corn. It is sometimes known as cornstarch and is used for thickening.

'Cream cheese' There are some very good non-dairy alternatives to cream cheese made from soya, some of which are flavoured with garlic or herbs. The unflavoured variety is used in the recipes featured here.

Dried fruits There is a long tradition in Greece of preserving the summer bounty of fresh fruit for use in the winter by drying. Popular fruits for drying include figs, peaches, apples, apricots, grapes and pears. Orange and lemon peel is also candied, for use in cakes and breads. Sultanas are often combined with green vegetables and currants and raisins are regularly used in grain dishes and vegetable stuffings.

Dried mushrooms Highly regarded for their rich, intense flavour, dried mushrooms need to be reconstituted in warm water before use. Although expensive, they are only used in small quantities so a little goes a long way.

Filo pastry Used in both sweet and savoury recipes, filo pastry is simply made from flour, salt and water. It is best bought, either frozen or chilled, as it is difficult and time consuming to make. The sheets should be brushed before cooking with melted margarine for sweet dishes or olive oil for savoury ones.

Flower waters Rose and orange flower waters are used as essential flavourings in desserts, cakes and biscuits. Beware of imitations - authentic flower waters are distilled from real flowers.

Herbs Fresh and dried herbs are used in Greek cuisine and certain herbs are strongly associated with Greek mythology.

Basil The large, aromatic, scented leaves of the basil plant combine particularly well with aubergines and tomatoes. Fresh whole leaves are sometimes used as a garnish or as a flavourful addition to green salads. Sprigs of fresh basil are used by Greek Orthodox priests to sprinkle holy water over the congregation.

Bay leaves The bay tree is believed by many Greeks to be Apollo's creation and bay leaves, with their very distinct, strong, slightly bitter flavour, are commonly used to flavour soups, stews, casseroles and grain dishes.

Coriander This uniquely flavoured herb has been cultivated in Greece since ancient times. It is always used fresh, either as an ingredient or as a garnish. Dried coriander leaves should be avoided as the taste bears no comparison to the fresh variety.

Dill This feathery-leafed herb has a distinctive aniseed flavour and was used as a cure for hiccups by ancient Greeks. It is often combined with mint and goes particularly well with potatoes, spinach, cabbage and carrots.

Fennel The fresh feathery fronds of the herb, rather than the vegetable, fennel are sometimes used as a garnish.

Marjoram This tiny-leafed herb has a very distinct, aromatic flavour which combines very well with green vegetables.

Mint Pluto is believed to have transformed his beloved nymph 'Minthe' into this strongly flavoured, fragrant herb. Mint is used to flavour numerous dishes and dried mint is sometimes preferred for its strength of flavour. It is often combined with dill and fresh leaves may be used for garnishing or added to green salads.

Oregano One of the most commonly used herbs in Greek cooking, Greek oregano grows wild in the mountainous areas. An attractive, small-leafed herb, oregano has a natural affinity with tomato and aubergine.

Parsley This universally popular herb is used as an ingredient and for garnishing. Parsley combines well with other herbs and the flat leafed variety is favoured in Greece. Fresh parsley was traditionally made into celebratory crowns for the winners at athletic games.

Rosemary The pine-needle thin leaves of this strongly flavoured, sweet and fragrant herb are used to flavour various vegetable dishes, especially roasted vegetables. It grows wild throughout Greece, but Greeks think the best type comes from the dry hill slopes near the sea.

Thyme The smell of thyme fills the air in June in the mountainous areas of Greece, where it grows in profusion. This highly aromatic herb is commonly used in soups and various other savoury dishes.

Lemon juice Citrus fruits are widely grown in some parts of Greece and fresh lemon juice is added to numerous dips, dressings, sauces and other savoury dishes to give a desired sharp flavour.

Lentils All lentils are a rich source of protein, fibre, vitamins and minerals, Green and red varieties are favoured in Greece for soups, stews and salads.

Olive oil An intrinsic ingredient in Greek cuisine, both for cooking and for making dressings. There are countless varieties to choose from, all with varying tastes depending on the type of olive they are made from. Extra-virgin oil is considered to be best and it is also the most expensive. For a really authentic taste look for oils produced in Greece.

Olives Greece reputedly grows the greatest variety of olives in the world and they are one of the country's major exports. They are simply eaten as an appetiser, or used as an ingredient or to garnish various savoury dishes.

'Parmesan' An authentic-tasting vegan version made from soya can be bought in health food stores and some supermarkets. It is used as a garnish and in toppings for some savoury dishes.

Pasta Although most pasta is simply made from durum wheat and water, some varieties do contain eggs so always read the packet. As well as the more familiar shapes a particular Greek favourite is orzo, a rice-shaped pasta.

Pine kernels These tiny fragrant nuts are the seeds of a pine tree which is native to the Mediterranean area. Pine kernels have a sweet creamy taste that goes well in sweet and savoury dishes. They are often used for garnishing and their flavour is enhanced even more if they are lightly toasted before using.

Pistachio nuts These light-green flavourful nuts are sold in their split shells or ready shelled, either salted or unsalted. The unsalted variety is used as a filling in sweet pastries and bowls of nuts are often served as mezedes.

Rice White and brown long grain rice is frequently combined with other ingredients to make pilaffs, stuffings for vegetables, fillings for pies, salads, casseroles and sweet rice pudding, a popular dessert. Plainly cooked rice makes a good accompaniment for stews and casseroles.

Semolina A nutritious and versatile grain made from durum wheat, semolina is often used in cake recipes, as well as for making creamy desserts and halva, a Greek and Middle Eastern speciality.

Sesame seeds These tiny protein-packed seeds are a frequent ingredient in biscuit and bread recipes and are also sprinkled on breads and pastries before baking.

Soya milk Unsweetened soya milk has been used in both sweet and savoury recipes.

Spices As ground spices quickly go stale and lose their flavour, Greek cooks prefer to grind the whole spices where possible, as and when needed.

Aniseed The spice that gives the famous Greek ouzo its distinctive flavour. Aniseed is also used whole or crushed in various bread and cake recipes.

Black onion seeds These crunchy, black, pear-shaped seeds have a pleasant mild oniony flavour and are used in particular in bread recipes or for sprinkling on bread dough before baking.

Black pepper A universally popular seasoning for savoury dishes. Freshly ground black peppercorns are preferred.

Cardamom This pine-fragranced spice is available as pods, seeds or ground. The pods vary in colour but it is generally agreed that the green variety is the more flavourful and aromatic. The seeds are added to spiced pilaffs, while the ground spice gives Greek Christmas bread its distinctive flavour.

Cinnamon Used either as a stick or ground, cinnamon has a warm, comforting, sweet flavour which makes it a very versatile spice and one which is regularly used in sweet recipes as well as in various savoury dishes.

Cloves The dried buds of an evergreen tree are valued for their anaesthetic and antiseptic properties. Whole cloves are used in savoury rice dishes and for flavouring fruit salads, while ground cloves are used in various dessert and baking recipes.

Coriander The dried seed of a plant which belongs to the parsley family. Coriander seeds have a mild, sweet, orangey flavour which is enhanced when the seeds are crushed.

Cumin Used both as seeds and ground, cumin has a strong earthy flavour and is regularly used in savoury dishes from Northern Greece, especially those containing lentils.

Fennel seeds The dried seeds of a plant belonging to the parsley family. Fennel seeds impart an aniseed/licorice flavour which combines well with tomato.

Nutmeg The large aromatic, sweet and spicy seed of an evergreen tropical tree. Nutmeg is available as whole seeds or grated and special nutmeg graters can be bought to grate the whole seeds. Grated nutmeg is used to flavour some biscuits.

Paprika This ground dried pod of a sweet red pepper adds colour and a mild sweet flavour to savoury dishes, especially those containing tomatoes.

Saffron The most expensive of all the spices available, saffron consists of the dried stigmas of a variety of crocus. Luckily, only a small amount is needed to impart colour and a pungent, slightly bitter, yet aromatic taste, especially to rice dishes.

Split peas Traditionally used to make fava, a thick nourishing dip, split peas are highly nutritious and provide good amounts of protein, vitamins, minerals and fibre. Choose smooth, unwrinkled dried peas, as older ones tend to toughen and take longer to cook.

Sun-dried tomatoes Available dry, for reconstituting in water, or preserved in olive oil, ready to use, sun-dried tomatoes have a unique and intense flavour. A sun-dried tomato paste is also available, which has a more intense, richer flavour than tomato purée.

Sunflower oil This light, neutral-tasting oil is often used in cakes and biscuits and for making pastry. It is low in saturated fat and high in polyunsaturated fat.

Tahini A thick nutritious paste made from ground sesame seeds, tahini is rich in protein, calcium and B vitamins. It adds a distinctive flavour and creaminess to sweet and savoury dishes.

Textured vegetable protein A nutritious and versatile soya product which readily absorbs the flavours of other ingredients. The natural minced variety is used here in various savoury recipes.

Tinned tomatoes Crushed or chopped tinned plum tomatoes are regularly used in cooked dishes to add a strong tomato flavour and they are especially useful when ripe fresh tomatoes are unavailable.

Tomato purée Used to strengthen the flavour of and add colour to tomato-based dishes.

Vegetable stock Used in various savoury recipes, a good stock is indispensable in the Greek kitchen. It's worth making in bulk and freezing in measured quantities for use as required. To make a good vegetable stock, peel and chop a selection of vegetables such as carrots, courgettes, celery, onions, leeks, potatoes and peppers. Put them in a large pan and season with black pepper. Cover with water, bring to the boil, cover the pan and simmer for about 30 minutes. Strain the liquid off through a fine sieve.

Vinegar Balsamic and red and white wine vinegars are used in dressings and often added to soups, stews and casseroles where an acidic taste is required.

Vine leaves Fresh vine leaves can be bought in specialist groceries and these need to be soaked in boiling water before stuffing. Vine leaves packed in brine are more readily available and these should be thoroughly washed in warm water to remove the salt before use.

Walnuts A rich source of polyunsaturated fats, studies have shown that walnuts have positive health benefits by helping to lower cholesterol levels. They are used as an ingredient and as a garnish for savoury dishes and in numerous baking and dessert recipes.

Wheat berries Husked whole wheat grains, commonly called berries, are rich in protein, vitamins and minerals. Wheat berries are sometimes combined with other grains and served as an accompaniment. They need to be soaked in water for 2 hours to soften before cooking.

Wine Several types of wine are produced from the various grapes that are grown in the major wine-producing areas of Attica, Macedonia and the Peloponnese. Many savoury dishes include a dash of red or white wine and it is also occasionally added to fruit salads.

Yeast Easy-blend dried yeast is used in the recipes here. It does not need to be reconstituted in liquid.

Yoghurt A vital ingredient in Greek cuisine, yoghurt is regularly used in both sweet and savoury recipes and plain soya yoghurt is an excellent substitute.

MEZEDES

Savoury little dishes known as mezedes are an integral part of Greek cuisine and are believed to have been served in the region since antiquity. Certainly today this tradition carries on and bars and tavernas all over Greece serve a selection of tasty little morsels to accompany drinks. They are also used as appetisers for main courses and they make ideal buffet foods. As well as the following dishes, bowls of olives and any of the salads from the salad section can be served as mezedes.

Dolmades (makes 24)

8oz/225g packet of preserved vine leaves

4oz/100g long grain rice

1 onion, peeled and finely chopped

1oz/25g raisins, chopped

1oz/25g pine kernels

juice of 1 lemon

9 fl.oz/250ml vegetable stock

1 tablespoon finely chopped fresh dill

1 tablespoon finely chopped fresh mint

¼ teaspoon ground cinnamon

black pepper

1 dessertspoon olive oil

3 tablespoons olive oil

1 garlic clove, crushed

lemon wedges

Wash the vine leaves thoroughly in warm water to remove the brine, then pat them dry with kitchen paper. Cut off any stems from the leaves and discard.

Heat the dessertspoonful of oil and fry the onion until soft. Add the rice and stir around for 30 seconds, then the vegetable stock, cinnamon, raisins and half of the lemon juice. Stir well, bring to the boil, cover and simmer gently until the liquid has been absorbed. Remove from the heat and add the pine kernels, dill and mint. Season with black pepper and mix thoroughly.

Lay out 24 vine leaves shiny side down and place a dessertspoonful of filling near the base of each leaf. Fold the two sides towards the centre, then roll the leaves up to enclose the filling. Line the base of a large heavy pan with vine leaves and fill the pan with the dolmades, packing them tightly together. Mix the remaining lemon juice with the remaining oil and the garlic and spoon evenly over the stuffed leaves. Pour in enough water to cover, then put an inverted plate on top to prevent the leaves moving or opening. Bring to the boil, place a lid on the pan and simmer very gently for 1 hour. Check the water regularly and keep topped up as necessary. Towards the end of the cooking time the liquid should be allowed to evaporate. Let the dolmades cool, then put them in the fridge until cold. Line a serving plate with any remaining vine leaves and arrange the dolmades on top. Garnish with lemon wedges to serve.

Walnut-stuffed mushrooms (makes 16)

16 medium-sized mushrooms, wiped

2oz/50g walnuts, grated

1oz/25g breadcrumbs

1 tablespoon vegan 'Parmesan'

1 garlic clove, crushed

1 dessertspoon olive oil

2 tablespoons white wine

1 teaspoon dried oregano

black pepper

extra olive oil

Finely chop the stalks from the mushroom and fry them with the garlic in the dessertspoonful of oil until the juices run. Remove from the heat and add the walnuts, breadcrumbs, 'Parmesan', wine and oregano. Season with black pepper and mix thoroughly until everything binds together. Brush the outsides of the mushroom caps with olive oil and fill each one with some of the filling, pressing it neatly to form a mound on top. Place the filled mushrooms in an oiled baking dish and bake in a preheated oven at 180°C/350°F/Gas mark 4 for 15-20 minutes until tender. Serve warm or cold.

Stuffed tomatoes (serves 6)

6 tomatoes, each approx. 3oz/75g

2oz/50g bulgar wheat

1 garlic clove, crushed

1 dessertspoon olive oil

4 tablespoons water

1 dessertspoon lemon juice

1 teaspoon dried mint

black pepper

extra olive oil

vegan 'Parmesan'

Cut each tomato in half, scoop out the centres and place the tomato shells in an oiled baking dish. Chop the scooped out centres. Briefly fry the garlic in the dessertspoonful of oil, then add the chopped tomato and any juice and the bulgar wheat, water, lemon juice and mint. Season with black pepper and stir well. Bring to the boil, cover and simmer for 1 minute. Remove from the heat and leave for 15 minutes, then fill each tomato shell with some of the mixture and drizzle a little olive oil on top. Sprinkle with 'Parmesan' and bake in a preheated oven at 180°C/350°F/Gas mark 4 for 15 minutes. Serve at room temperature.

Aubergine and almond croquettes (makes 12)

12oz/350g aubergine

3oz/75g ground almonds

3oz/75g breadcrumbs

1 onion, peeled and grated

1 garlic clove, crushed

1 rounded tablespoon vegan 'Parmesan'

1 rounded teaspoon dried oregano

black pepper

flour

olive oil

Make a few slits in the aubergine with a sharp knife and bake it in a preheated oven at 180°C/350°F/Gas mark 4 for about 30 minutes until soft. Carefully remove the skin and discard. Mash the flesh, then add the ground almonds, breadcrumbs, onion, garlic, 'Parmesan' and oregano. Season with black pepper and mix well. Add a little flour to bind and shape heaped dessertspoonfuls of the mixture into croquettes with damp hands. Roll each croquette in flour and put them on a plate. Cover and chill for 2 hours. Shallow fry the croquettes in hot olive oil, turning occasionally, until golden brown. Drain on kitchen paper and serve with a salad garnish and a yoghurt dressing.

Spinach pizzettes (makes 8)

bases

8oz/225g plain flour

1 teaspoon easy-blend yeast

½ teaspoon salt

1 tablespoon olive oil

approx. 4 fl.oz/125ml warm water

topping

12oz/350g fresh spinach

1 medium onion, peeled and grated

1 garlic clove, crushed

1 dessertspoon olive oil

black pepper

chopped green olives

grated vegan 'cheese'

extra olive oil

Mix the flour with the yeast and salt in a large bowl. Stir in the olive oil and gradually add the water until a soft dough forms. Knead the dough well, then return it to the bowl, cover and leave in a warm place for 1 hour. Knead the dough again and divide it into 8 equal pieces. Shape each piece into a round of 3 inches/8cm diameter. Place the circles on a greased baking sheet and leave in a warm place for 30 minutes.

Wash the spinach leaves and put them in a saucepan with only the water that clings to them. Cook gently until tender, then drain and allow to cool before squeezing out all excess liquid. Chop the spinach finely. Fry the onion and garlic in the dessertspoonful of oil until soft. Remove from the heat and add the spinach, season with black pepper and mix well. Brush the pizzette bases with olive oil and spoon the spinach mixture evenly on top. Drizzle a little olive oil over the spinach, then bake in a preheated oven at 200°C/400°F/Gas mark 6 for 12-15 minutes. Garnish with chopped olives and grated 'cheese' and serve warm.

Vegetable kebabs (serves 4)

1lb/450g mixed vegetables (e.g. a selection of aubergine, courgette, mushroom, tomato, onion, pepper)

marinade

1 small red onion, peeled and grated

1 garlic clove, crushed

1 tablespoon olive oil

1 tablespoon lemon juice

1 rounded teaspoon dried oregano

black pepper

1 bay leaf

Cut the vegetables into even-sized chunks and put them in a mixing bowl. Combine the marinade ingredients and add to the vegetables. Mix thoroughly, then cover and refrigerate for a couple of hours.

Thread the vegetables onto small square skewers and place them under a hot grill, turning occasionally, for about 20 minutes until tender.

Gyros (serves 8)

8 mini pitta breads

shredded lettuce

tomato slices

tsatsiki (see page 93)

2oz/50g natural minced textured vegetable protein

2oz/50g breadcrumbs

2oz/50g ground almonds

1oz/25g flour

1 onion, peeled and finely chopped

1 garlic clove, crushed

10 fl.oz/300ml vegetable stock

1 dessertspoon olive oil

1 dessertspoon tomato purée

1 rounded teaspoon ground cumin

black pepper

extra flour

extra olive oil

Fry the onion and garlic in the dessertspoonful of oil for 5 minutes. Add the vegetable protein, cumin, vegetable stock and tomato purée and stir well. Bring to the boil, cover and simmer for 10 minutes. Uncover and simmer for another 5 minutes, stirring regularly, until all the liquid has been absorbed. Remove from the heat and add the breadcrumbs, almonds and 1oz/25g flour, season with black pepper and mix very well. Divide the mixture into 8 equal portions and with wet hands shape each one into a flat oval. Dip these in flour, pat off excess and put them on a plate, then cover and keep in the fridge for 2 hours. Shallow fry the patties in hot olive oil for a few minutes on each side until golden and drain on kitchen paper. Warm the pitta breads and split them open. Fill each bread with one of the patties, a little shredded lettuce and a tomato slice, and top with a little tsatsiki.

Kalamata paste (serves 4)

6oz/175g kalamata olives

2 tablespoons lemon juice

2 tablespoons olive oil

2 garlic cloves, crushed

1 dessertspoon white wine vinegar

1 rounded teaspoon dried oregano

black pepper

Blend the ingredients together until smooth. Spread onto warm bread to serve.

Fava (serves 4/6)

6oz/175g split yellow peas

1 onion, peeled and finely chopped

1 garlic clove, crushed

1 tablespoon olive oil

1 tablespoon lemon juice

1 rounded teaspoon dried parsley

black pepper

Soak the split peas in water overnight. Drain and put them in a pan of fresh water. Bring to the boil, cover and simmer for about 1 hour until the peas are soft. Drain again and mash or blend the peas to a purée with 3 tablespoonfuls of the cooking liquid.

Heat the oil and fry the onion and garlic until soft. Add the pea purée, lemon juice and parsley and season with black pepper. Mix thoroughly, then transfer to a serving bowl and use as a dip or spread onto bread.

Chickpea-filled filo rolls (makes 12)

10oz/300g filo pastry

olive oil

sesame seeds

filling

1lb/450g cooked chickpeas, mashed

2oz/50g vegan 'cheese', grated

1 onion, peeled and finely chopped

2 garlic cloves, crushed

1 tablespoon olive oil

2 tablespoons lemon juice

2 rounded tablespoons finely chopped fresh parsley

black pepper

Fry the onion and garlic in the tablespoonful of oil until softened. Remove from the heat and add the mashed chickpeas, 'cheese', lemon juice and parsley, season with black pepper and combine well.

Cut the filo pastry into 24 sheets of about 9 x 5 inches/23 x 13cm. Place 12 sheets on a flat surface and brush them with olive oil. Put another sheet of filo on top of each one, then divide the filling between the oblongs, placing it on the bottom one-third of the pastry. Fold the two long edges of each oblong towards the centre to cover the edges of the filling, then roll the pastry up to enclose the filling completely. Arrange the rolls in an oiled baking dish and brush them with olive oil. Sprinkle with sesame seeds and bake in a preheated oven at 180°C/350°F/Gas mark 4 for 20-25 minutes until golden brown.

Marinated peppers with 'cheese' (serves 4)

4oz/100g red pepper

4oz/100g green pepper

4oz/100g vegan 'cheese', diced

1 small red onion, peeled and finely chopped

2 garlic cloves, crushed

6 olives, chopped

1 teaspoon dried thyme

black pepper

2 tablespoons olive oil

1 dessertspoon lemon juice

1 dessertspoon balsamic vinegar

Grill the peppers until the skins blister all over. Carefully remove the skins, membranes and seeds and chop the flesh. Put this in a large bowl with the 'cheese', onion, garlic and olives. Mix the olive oil with the lemon juice, vinegar and thyme and season with black pepper. Pour over the pepper mixture and toss well. Spoon into a serving bowl, cover and chill for a few hours before serving.

Aubergine and tomato appetiser (serves 4)

12oz/350g aubergine, finely chopped

6oz/175g tomato, skinned and finely chopped

1 small red onion, peeled and grated

2 garlic cloves, crushed

3 tablespoons olive oil

1 rounded teaspoon coriander seeds, crushed

1 teaspoon dried parsley

1 dessertspoon lemon juice

black pepper

Fry the aubergine, onion and garlic in the oil, stirring frequently, for about 15 minutes until soft. Remove from the heat and add the remaining ingredients. Mash the mixture, transfer to a bowl and serve at room temperature.

Roasted nuts and seeds (serves 4/6)

4oz/100g mixed shelled pistachios and sunflower and pumpkin seeds

1 dessertspoon sunflower oil

black pepper

Mix the nuts and seeds with the oil and fry over a medium heat for a few minutes until they begin to turn golden, making sure you keep them moving to prevent burning. Season with black pepper and put into a dish. Serve warm or cold.

Chickpea and sesame dip (serves 4)

8oz/225g cooked chickpeas, mashed

2 rounded tablespoons light tahini

2 tablespoons lemon juice

2 tablespoons water

1 tablespoon olive oil

1 garlic clove, crushed

1 teaspoon dried parsley

black pepper

toasted sesame seeds

Mix the chickpeas with the tahini, lemon juice, water, oil, garlic and parsley. Season with black pepper and garnish with toasted sesame seeds before serving.

Baked aubergine and tomato rings (serves 4)

12oz/350g aubergine, cut into ½ inch/1cm slices

8oz/225g tomatoes, skinned and sliced

olive oil

dried oregano

black pepper

grated vegan 'cheese'

Brush the aubergine slices on both sides with olive oil and place them in an oiled baking dish. Bake in a preheated oven at 180°C/350°F/Gas mark 4 for 15 minutes. Turn the slices of aubergine over and arrange the tomato slices on top of them. Drizzle with a little olive oil and sprinkle with oregano. Season with black pepper and return to the oven for about 15 minutes until the aubergine is tender. Serve warm, garnished with grated 'cheese'.

Savoury patties (makes 12)

2oz/50g natural minced textured vegetable protein

2oz/50g breadcrumbs

2oz/50g walnuts, grated

1oz/25g vegan 'cheese', grated

1 onion, peeled and finely chopped

1 garlic clove, crushed

10 fl.oz/300ml vegetable stock

1 rounded dessertspoon tomato purée

1 dessertspoon lemon juice

1 dessertspoon olive oil

1 rounded teaspoon dried oregano

½ teaspoon paprika

black pepper

flour

extra olive oil

Fry the onion and garlic in the dessertspoonful of oil until soft. Add the vegetable protein, stock, tomato purée, lemon juice, oregano and paprika and stir well. Bring to the boil, cover and simmer for 10 minutes, then uncover and continue simmering for about 5 minutes while stirring, until all the liquid has been absorbed. Remove from the heat and add the breadcrumbs, walnuts and 'cheese', season with black pepper and mix thoroughly. Take rounded dessertspoonfuls of the mixture and roll into balls. Roll these in flour until completely covered, then flatten each ball slightly and put them on a plate. Cover and refrigerate for 2 hours. Shallow fry the patties in hot olive oil for a few minutes on each side until browned. Drain on kitchen paper and serve warm or cold with a salad garnish.

Skordalia (serves 4)

12oz/350g potatoes, peeled

3 garlic cloves, crushed

3 tablespoons olive oil

1 tablespoon lemon juice

1 tablespoon white wine vinegar

black pepper

Cut the potatoes into even-sized chunks and boil them, then drain and dry off over a low heat. Mash the potatoes, add the garlic, oil, lemon juice and vinegar, season with black pepper and mix well until smooth. Add a little water, if necessary, to make a thick dipping consistency, then spoon into a serving bowl and serve at room temperature.

Mushroom and walnut pittes (makes 12)

10oz/300g filo pastry

olive oil

sesame seeds

filling

12oz/350g mushrooms, wiped and finely chopped

1 onion, peeled and finely chopped

2 garlic cloves, crushed

2oz/50g walnuts, grated

2oz/50g breadcrumbs

1 rounded tablespoon vegan 'Parmesan'

1 tablespoon olive oil

1 dessertspoon dried parsley

1 teaspoon dried dill

black pepper

Fry the onion and garlic in the oil until softened, then add the mushrooms and fry until the juices begin to run. Remove from the heat and mix in the remaining filling ingredients.

Cut the filo pastry into 24 sheets of approximately 9 x 5 inches/23 x 13cm. Spread 12 sheets out on a flat surface, brush them with olive oil and put another sheet on top of each one. Divide the filling between the 12 pastry oblongs, placing it on the bottom half only. Fold the right hand corner over to the left, then fold the pastry up and then to the right, tucking the edges in as you go, making triangles. Arrange these on a greased baking sheet, brush them with olive oil and sprinkle with sesame seeds. Bake in a preheated oven at 180°C/350°F/Gas mark 4 for 20-25 minutes until golden. Serve warm.

Savoury stuffed pittas (makes 8)

8 mini round pitta breads

shredded crisp lettuce

plain soya yoghurt

filling

9oz/250g aubergine, finely chopped

4oz/100g tomato, skinned and chopped

1oz/25g natural minced textured vegetable protein

1 onion, peeled and finely chopped

1 garlic clove, crushed

3 tablespoons olive oil

1 dessertspoon tomato purée

6 fl.oz/175ml vegetable stock

1 teaspoon dried oregano

½ teaspoon dried basil

black pepper

Fry the aubergine, onion and garlic in the oil for 15 minutes, stirring frequently to prevent sticking. Add the remaining filling ingredients and stir well, then bring to the boil, cover and simmer for 10 minutes. Uncover and continue simmering for 10 minutes more, stirring occasionally, until the liquid has been absorbed and the mixture is thick.

Warm the pitta breads and slit them open. Put some shredded lettuce in each pitta and divide the filling between them. Garnish with a little plain yoghurt.

Courgette fritters (makes 12)

8oz/225g courgette, grated

1 onion, peeled and grated

1 garlic clove, crushed

2oz/50g breadcrumbs

2oz/50g flour

1 rounded tablespoon vegan 'Parmesan'

1 rounded teaspoon dried parsley

black pepper

olive oil

Mix the courgettes, onion and garlic in a large bowl, add the breadcrumbs, flour, 'Parmesan' and parsley and season with black pepper. Combine thoroughly until the mixture sticks together. Take rounded dessertspoonfuls of this mixture and loosely shape them into ovals. Shallow fry these for a few minutes on each side in olive oil until golden brown. Drain on kitchen paper and serve warm with a salad garnish.

Aubergine dip (serves 4)

1lb/450g aubergine

1 garlic clove, crushed

1 rounded dessertspoon light tahini

1 dessertspoon lemon juice

1 dessertspoon olive oil

4 tablespoons water

½ teaspoon dried parsley

black pepper

Cut the aubergine in half lengthwise and place under a hot grill, turning occasionally, until soft. Scoop out the flesh and blend smooth with the remaining ingredients. Transfer to a serving bowl and serve at room temperature.

Tiropita (makes 12)

10oz/300g filo pastry

olive oil

black onion seeds

filling

4oz/100g vegan 'cream cheese'

4oz/100g vegan 'cheese', grated

1 onion, peeled and finely chopped

1 dessertspoon olive oil

6 fl.oz/175ml soya milk

2 rounded tablespoons cornflour

1 dessertspoon dried parsley

black pepper

Fry the onion in the oil until soft. Remove from the heat and add the 'cream cheese' and grated 'cheese', mixing well. Dissolve the cornflour in the soya milk and add to the pan together with the parsley. Season with black pepper and stir thoroughly until well combined. Bring to the boil while stirring and continue stirring for a minute or two until the sauce is thick. Remove from the heat and allow to cool.

Cut the filo pastry into 24 sheets of about 9 x 5 inches/23 x 13cm. Spread 12 sheets out on a flat surface, brush with olive oil and put another sheet on top of each one. Divide the filling between the 12 oblongs, placing it neatly at one end. Fold the two long sides in towards the centre, then roll each oblong up to enclose the filling completely. Arrange the parcels on an oiled baking sheet and brush them with olive oil. Sprinkle with black onion seeds and bake in a preheated oven at 180°C/350°F/Gas mark 4 for 20-25 minutes until browned. Serve warm.

SOUPS

Typically made from wholesome mixtures of fresh vegetables, pulses and pasta, Greek soups are just as likely to be served with accompaniments as satisfying light meals as they are to be starters for the main course. As with many Greek dishes, flavourings vary from the lightly spiced varieties popular in the north of the country to the herby Mediterranean flavours found in the south. Suitable accompaniments for soup to make it into a light meal include grain dishes, breads and salads.

Chickpea soup (serves 4)

1lb/450g cooked chickpeas

1 onion, peeled and finely chopped

2 garlic cloves, crushed

2 tablespoons olive oil

20 fl.oz/600ml vegetable stock

1 dessertspoon finely chopped fresh rosemary

black pepper

1 tablespoon lemon juice

finely chopped fresh parsley

Heat the oil in a large pan and fry the onion and garlic until soft. Slip the skins from the chickpeas and discard. Add the chickpeas to the pan together with the vegetable stock and rosemary, season with black pepper and bring to the boil. Cover and simmer for 15 minutes, stirring occasionally. Break up the chickpeas slightly by mashing, then stir in the lemon juice, ladle the soup into bowls and serve garnished with chopped parsley.

Green lentil and vegetable soup (serves 4)

8oz/225g potatoes, peeled and diced

6oz/175g leek, trimmed and sliced

6oz/175g tomatoes, skinned and chopped

4oz/100g green lentils

2oz/50g mushrooms, wiped and sliced

1 onion, peeled and chopped

2 garlic cloves, crushed

1 tablespoon olive oil

1 rounded tablespoon finely chopped fresh coriander

1 rounded teaspoon ground cumin

1 bay leaf

black pepper

25 fl.oz/750ml boiling vegetable stock

extra chopped fresh coriander

Wash the lentils, then soak them in the stock for an hour. Heat the oil in a large pan and fry the leek, onion and garlic for 5 minutes. Add the cumin and tomatoes and fry for another 2 minutes, then put in the lentils and the soaking stock together with the potatoes, mushrooms, coriander and bay leaf. Season with black pepper and stir well. Bring to the boil, cover and simmer, stirring occasionally, for about 40 minutes until the lentils are done and the soup is thick. Garnish with chopped coriander when serving.

Onion soup (serves 4)

1lb/450g onions, peeled and chopped

8oz/225g potatoes, peeled and diced

2 garlic cloves, crushed

2 tablespoons olive oil

20 fl.oz/600ml vegetable stock

1 bay leaf

1 sprig of fresh thyme

black pepper

2 rounded tablespoons plain soya yoghurt

chopped fresh parsley

Fry the onion and garlic in the olive oil for 10 minutes. Add the potato, stock, bay leaf and thyme and season with black pepper, stir well and bring to the boil. Cover and simmer for 15 minutes, then take off the heat and remove the thyme. Mash the soup lightly to break up the potato and stir in the yoghurt. Ladle into serving bowls and garnish with parsley.

Red lentil and carrot soup (serves 4)

4oz/100g red lentils

4oz/100g carrot, scraped and finely chopped

4oz/100g tomato, skinned and chopped

1 onion, peeled and finely chopped

1 garlic clove, crushed

24 fl.oz/725ml vegetable stock

1 dessertspoon olive oil

1 dessertspoon tomato purée

1 teaspoon dried parsley

½ teaspoon paprika

1 bay leaf

black pepper

1 dessertspoon red wine vinegar

Soften the onion and garlic in the oil in a large pan. Add the tomato and cook until pulpy, then the remaining ingredients, apart from the vinegar, and stir well. Bring to the boil, cover and simmer gently for 35-40 minutes until the lentils are soft. Stir in the vinegar just before serving.

Country soup (serves 4)

6oz/175g potato, peeled and diced

6oz/175g carrot, scraped and finely chopped

6oz/175g courgette, chopped

6oz/175g tomatoes, skinned and chopped

4oz/100g leek, trimmed and sliced

1 red onion, peeled and chopped

1 garlic clove, crushed

14 fl.oz/425ml vegetable stock

1 tablespoon tomato purée

1 tablespoon olive oil

1 bay leaf

1 sprig of fresh thyme

½ teaspoon paprika

black pepper

1 tablespoon balsamic vinegar

grated vegan 'cheese'

Heat the oil in a large pan and fry the leek, onion and garlic for 5 minutes. Add the remaining ingredients, except the vinegar and 'cheese', and stir well. Bring to the boil, cover and simmer, stirring occasionally, for about 20 minutes until the vegetables are tender and the soup is thick. Stir in the vinegar, ladle the soup into serving bowls and sprinkle with grated 'cheese'.

Fassolada (serves 4)

8oz/225g cooked haricot beans

8oz/225g potatoes, peeled and finely diced

4oz/100g carrot, scraped and finely diced

4oz/100g tomato, skinned and chopped

2oz/50g red pepper, chopped

1 onion, peeled and chopped

1 celery stick, trimmed and finely sliced

1 garlic clove, crushed

1 tablespoon olive oil

1 dessertspoon tomato purée

15 fl.oz/450ml vegetable stock

1 dessertspoon finely chopped fresh oregano

1 dessertspoon finely chopped fresh thyme

black pepper

1oz/25g black olives, sliced

grated vegan 'cheese'

finely chopped fresh parsley

Mash or blend half of the beans with 5 fl.oz/150ml of the stock. Heat the oil in a large pan and fry the onion, celery and garlic until soft, then add the tomato and cook until pulpy. Stir in the remaining stock, potato, carrot, red pepper, tomato purée, oregano and thyme, season with black pepper and bring to the boil. Cover and simmer, stirring occasionally, for 15 minutes. Add the blended bean mixture together with the remaining beans and the olives. Bring back to the boil and simmer for 5-10 minutes more until the vegetables are done. Serve in bowls, garnished with grated 'cheese' and chopped parsley.

Tomato and pasta soup (serves 4)

1lb/450g ripe tomatoes, skinned and chopped

2oz/50g tiny pasta shapes

1 red onion, peeled and finely chopped

2 garlic cloves, crushed

1 tablespoon olive oil

1 tablespoon tomato purée

20 fl.oz/600ml vegetable stock

2 tablespoons finely chopped fresh basil

1 bay leaf

black pepper

vegan 'Parmesan'

Fry the onion and garlic in the oil in a large pan until softened, then add the tomatoes and cook until pulpy. Remove from the heat and mash until smooth. Return to the heat and stir in the pasta, tomato purée, stock, basil and bay leaf. Season with black pepper and bring to the boil. Cover and simmer, stirring occasionally, for 15 minutes. Ladle the soup into serving bowls and sprinkle with 'Parmesan' to serve.

Sesame and potato soup (serves 4)

12oz/350g potatoes, peeled and finely chopped

1 onion, peeled and finely chopped

1 garlic clove, crushed

1 tablespoon olive oil

2 tablespoons lemon juice

2 rounded tablespoons light tahini

24 fl.oz/725ml vegetable stock

1 dessertspoon dried parsley

black pepper

2 rounded tablespoons plain soya yoghurt

toasted sesame seeds

Soften the onion and garlic in the oil in a large saucepan. Add the potato, lemon juice, tahini, stock and parsley and season with black pepper. Stir well and bring to the boil, then cover and simmer gently, stirring occasionally, for about 20 minutes until the potato is cooked. Transfer half of the soup to a blender and blend smooth. Pour back into the rest of the soup in the pan and add the yoghurt. Mix thoroughly, then ladle the soup into serving bowls and garnish with toasted sesame seeds.

Aubergine and orzo soup (serves 4)

8oz/225g aubergine, finely chopped

6oz/175g ripe tomatoes, skinned and chopped

2oz/50g orzo

1 red onion, peeled and finely chopped

1 garlic clove, crushed

2 tablespoons olive oil

1 dessertspoon tomato purée

1 tablespoon finely chopped fresh basil

½ teaspoon paprika

1 bay leaf

black pepper

20 fl.oz/600ml vegetable stock

vegan 'Parmesan'

toasted pine kernels

Fry the aubergine, onion and garlic in the oil in a large pan for 10 minutes, stirring frequently to prevent sticking. Add the tomatoes and cook for 5 minutes more, stirring occasionally. Stir in the stock, orzo, tomato purée, basil, paprika and bay leaf and season with black pepper. Bring to the boil, cover and simmer for 15 minutes, stirring occasionally. Serve garnished with 'Parmesan' and pine kernels.

Mushroom, pepper and bean soup (serves 4)

6oz/175g mushrooms, wiped and chopped

6oz/175g mixed peppers, chopped

6oz/175g cooked mixed beans

¼ oz/7g dried mushrooms

1 onion, peeled and finely chopped

1 garlic clove, crushed

1 tablespoon olive oil

1 teaspoon ground cumin

1 teaspoon coriander seeds, crushed

black pepper

10 fl.oz/300ml boiling water

4 fl.oz/125ml soya milk

1 rounded dessertspoon cornflour

1 rounded tablespoon plain soya yoghurt

finely chopped fresh coriander

Soak the dried mushrooms in the boiling water for 30 minutes. Fry the peppers, onion and garlic in the oil for 5 minutes, stirring occasionally, then add the mushrooms, cumin and crushed coriander seeds and stir around for 2 minutes. Stir in the mushrooms and soaking water together with the beans, season with black pepper and bring to the boil. Cover and simmer for about 10 minutes until the peppers are tender. Dissolve the cornflour in the soya milk and add to the pan. Bring the soup back to the boil while stirring and simmer for a minute or so until it thickens. Remove from the heat and stir in the yoghurt. Ladle the soup into bowls and garnish with chopped coriander.

Split pea and pepper soup (serves 4)

10oz/300g mixed peppers, chopped

4oz/100g split yellow peas

1 onion, peeled and finely chopped

1 garlic clove, crushed

1 tablespoon olive oil

1 tablespoon lemon juice

1 tablespoon finely chopped fresh parsley

1 tablespoon finely chopped fresh oregano

1 bay leaf

black pepper

1 rounded tablespoon plain soya yoghurt

fresh parsley sprigs

Soak the split peas in water overnight. Drain and bring them to the boil in fresh water. Cover and simmer for about 1 hour until the peas are soft, keeping the water topped up. Drain the cooking liquid into a measuring jug and make up to 12 fl.oz/350ml with water, if necessary. Mash the peas until smooth. Fry the peppers, onion and garlic in the oil for 10 minutes in a large pan, stirring occasionally. Remove from the heat and add the mashed peas, measured cooking liquid, lemon juice, chopped parsley and oregano and the bay leaf. Season with black pepper and stir well, then bring to the boil. Cover and simmer, stirring occasionally, for 10 minutes. Remove from the heat and stir in the yoghurt. Garnish each bowl of soup with a sprig of parsley when serving.

MAIN COURSES

The custom of avoiding meat and dairy products during Lent and on various religious days throughout the year is still observed today by many members of the Greek Orthodox Church. A whole host of dishes for these occasions based instead on grains, pulses, pasta and fresh seasonal vegetables is the result. Stews, casseroles and savoury pies are particular favourites, as are stuffed vegetables, a legacy of the Turkish invaders. In many rural areas the main meal is eaten at midday and it is often followed by a siesta.

Moussaka (serves 4)

base

1lb/450g aubergine, diced

1 onion, peeled and chopped

2 garlic cloves, crushed

4oz/100g button mushrooms, wiped and halved

2oz/50g natural minced textured vegetable protein

10oz/300g ripe tomatoes, skinned and chopped

4 tablespoons olive oil

2 tablespoons red wine

1 tablespoon tomato purée

9 fl.oz/250ml vegetable stock

black pepper

1 bay leaf

1 rounded tablespoon finely chopped fresh basil

1 rounded tablespoon finely chopped fresh oregano

pinch of ground cinnamon

topping

1lb/450g potatoes, peeled and thinly sliced

5 fl.oz/150ml soya milk

¼oz/7g cornflour

1oz/25g vegan 'cheese', grated

1 rounded tablespoon plain soya yoghurt

chopped fresh parsley

Heat the oil in a large pan and fry the aubergine, onion and garlic for 15 minutes, stirring frequently to prevent sticking. Add the remaining base ingredients apart from the mushrooms, bring to the boil, cover and simmer for 5 minutes. Add the mushrooms and continue simmering for another 5 minutes, stirring frequently. Spoon the mixture into a shallow casserole dish.

Boil the potato slices for 5 minutes, then drain and arrange them on top of the vegetables. Mix the cornflour with the soya milk until smooth and pour it into a small saucepan. Add the 'cheese' and bring to the boil while stirring. Continue stirring for a few seconds until the sauce thickens. Remove from the heat, stir in the yoghurt and spoon the sauce evenly over the potatoes. Bake in a preheated oven at 180°C/350°F/Gas mark 4 for about 30 minutes until browned. Garnish with chopped fresh parsley and serve with a green salad and warm bread.

Stuffed peppers (serves 4)

4 peppers (each approx. 6oz/175g)

4oz/100g long grain rice

1oz/25g natural minced textured vegetable protein

6 spring onions, trimmed and finely sliced

2 garlic cloves, crushed

1oz/25g currants

1oz/25g pine kernels

16 fl.oz/475ml vegetable stock

1 dessertspoon olive oil

1 tablespoon finely chopped fresh dill

1 tablespoon finely chopped fresh parsley

pinch of ground cinnamon

black pepper

1 dessertspoon tomato purée

2 tablespoons water

Blanch the whole peppers in boiling water for 3 minutes. Drain and allow to cool, then slice off the tops and remove the membranes and seeds. Arrange the peppers upright in a greased baking dish, making sure they are tightly packed.

Heat the oil and fry the spring onions and garlic. Add the rice and stir around for a few seconds, then stir in the vegetable protein, currants, stock, dill, parsley and cinnamon and season with black pepper. Bring to the boil, cover and simmer gently until the liquid has been absorbed. Remove from the heat and stir in the pine kernels. Spoon the mixture into the peppers and place the lids on top. Mix the tomato purée with the water and pour over the peppers. Cover the dish tightly with foil and bake in a preheated oven at 180°C/350°F/Gas mark 4 for about 45 minutes until the peppers are tender. Allow to cool, then serve at room temperature with bread and vegetables or salad.

Spaghetti with sun-dried tomato and vegetable sauce (serves 4)

8oz/225g spaghetti

14oz/400g tin chopped tomatoes

8oz/225g courgette, chopped

6oz/175g mixed peppers, chopped

1oz/25g sun-dried tomatoes, finely chopped

1 large red onion, peeled and finely chopped

2 garlic cloves, crushed

2 tablespoons olive oil

4 tablespoons water

1 tablespoon lemon juice

1 bay leaf

1 teaspoon dried thyme

black pepper

grated vegan 'cheese'

chopped black olives

Soak the sun-dried tomatoes in 1 tablespoonful of oil for 2 hours. Heat the other tablespoonful of oil in a large saucepan and fry the onion and garlic until soft. Add the sun-dried and tinned tomatoes, courgette, peppers, water, lemon juice, bay leaf and thyme, season with black pepper and stir well. Bring to the boil, cover and simmer, stirring occasionally, for about 15 minutes until the vegetables are done. Meanwhile, cook the spaghetti until just tender. Drain and add to the hot sauce. Toss thoroughly, then spoon onto plates and garnish with the 'cheese' and olives. Serve with warm bread and salad accompaniments.

Spinach, leek and mushroom pie (serves 4/6)

10oz/300g filo pastry

olive oil

sesame seeds

 filling

1lb/450g fresh spinach

1lb/450g leeks, trimmed and sliced

8oz/225g mushrooms, wiped and chopped

2oz/50g vegan 'cheese', grated

1 garlic clove, crushed

1 tablespoon olive oil

1 rounded teaspoon dried mint

1 rounded teaspoon dried dill

black pepper

Wash the spinach leaves and put them in a pan with only the water that clings to them. Cover and cook gently until tender. Allow to cool slightly, then squeeze out excess water and chop the spinach finely.

Soften the leek and garlic in the oil. Add the mushrooms and fry for 2 minutes more. Remove from the heat and add the chopped spinach, grated 'cheese', mint and dill. Season with black pepper and mix very well.

Line a 9 inch/23cm greased deep loose-bottomed flan tin with a third of the filo sheets, brushing between each sheet with olive oil and leaving an overhang to fold over the filling. Spread half the filling into the lined flan case and press down evenly. Cover with half of the remaining filo sheets, again brushing between each sheet with olive oil. Spread the rest of the filling on top and fold the overhanging pastry over the filling. Finely shred the remaining filo sheets and scrunch them over the top to enclose the filling completely. Brush with olive oil and sprinkle with sesame seeds, then bake in a preheated oven at 180°C/350°F/Gas mark 4 for 25-30 minutes until golden brown. Carefully remove from the tin, cut into wedges and serve with a grain dish.

Spiced barley and vegetable stew (serves 4)

8oz/225g potatoes, peeled and diced

8oz/225g carrot, scraped and diced

8oz/225g leek, trimmed and sliced

4oz/100g green pepper, chopped

4oz/100g tomato, skinned and chopped

4oz/100g pot barley

2 garlic cloves, crushed

1 tablespoon olive oil

1 dessertspoon tomato purée

1 dessertspoon ground cumin

¼ teaspoon ground cinnamon

2 tablespoons finely chopped fresh coriander

black pepper

fresh coriander leaves

Soak the barley in boiling water for an hour, then bring to the boil, cover and simmer for 20 minutes. Drain the cooking liquid into a measuring jug and make up to 20 fl.oz/600ml with water.

Fry the leek and garlic in the oil for 5 minutes in a large pan. Add the tomato, cumin and cinnamon and fry for another 2 minutes. Stir in the drained barley, potato, carrot, green pepper, tomato purée, chopped coriander and measured cooking liquid and season with black pepper. Bring to the boil, cover and simmer, stirring occasionally, for 30 minutes until the vegetables and barley are done. Transfer to a serving dish and garnish with coriander leaves. Serve with warm bread and a plain vegetable or salad.

Baked pasta with aubergine and cannellini beans (serves 4)

1lb/450g aubergine, diced

1 red onion, peeled and finely chopped

2 garlic cloves, crushed

14oz/400g tin chopped tomatoes

8oz/225g cooked cannellini beans

4oz/100g pasta spirals

7 fl.oz/200ml vegetable stock

4 tablespoons olive oil

1 tablespoon balsamic vinegar

1 rounded tablespoon finely chopped fresh basil

1 teaspoon fennel seeds

½ teaspoon paprika

black pepper

topping

1oz/25g breadcrumbs

1oz/25g pine kernels, chopped

1 rounded tablespoon vegan 'Parmesan'

fresh basil leaves

Heat the oil in a large pan and fry the aubergine, onion and garlic for 15 minutes, stirring frequently to prevent sticking. Remove from the heat and add the tomatoes, beans, stock, vinegar, basil, fennel seeds and paprika. Season with black pepper and mix well. Cook the pasta until just tender, drain and add to the sauce. Combine well and spoon into to a greased shallow baking dish. Mix the breadcrumbs with the pine kernels and 'Parmesan' and sprinkle evenly over the top. Cover with foil and bake in a preheated oven at 180°C/350°F/Gas mark 4 for 25 minutes, then remove the foil and bake for 5-10 minutes more until golden. Garnish with fresh basil leaves and serve with vegetable or salad accompaniments.

Bulgar-stuffed courgettes (serves 4)

4 courgettes (each approx. 8oz/225g)

filling

8oz/225g bulgar wheat

1 medium onion, peeled and finely chopped

2 garlic cloves, crushed

1 tablespoon olive oil

12 fl.oz/350ml hot vegetable stock

1 rounded teaspoon dried mint

black pepper

sauce

12oz/350g ripe tomatoes, peeled and chopped

1 small onion, peeled and finely chopped

1 garlic clove, crushed

1 tablespoon red wine vinegar

1 dessertspoon tomato purée

1 dessertspoon olive oil

1 teaspoon dried dill

½ teaspoon paprika

black pepper

grated vegan 'cheese'

Cut the courgettes in half lengthwise and scoop out the centres, leaving the shells about ¼ inch/5mm thick. Arrange the courgette shells in a greased baking dish and finely chop the scooped out flesh. Fry the onion and garlic for the filling in the oil until softened. Add the chopped courgette and fry for a further 2 minutes, then remove from the heat and add the bulgar wheat, stock and mint. Season with black pepper and stir well. Cover and leave to stand for 20 minutes until the liquid has been absorbed. Fill each courgette shell with some of the mixture and spoon any remaining mixture over the top.

Heat the oil for the sauce and fry the onion and garlic until soft. Add the tomatoes, vinegar, tomato purée, dill and paprika and season with black pepper, then bring to the boil and simmer for 5 minutes, stirring frequently. Spoon the sauce over the filled courgettes and cover the dish with foil. Bake in a preheated oven at 180°C/350°F/Gas mark 4 for about 35 minutes until the courgettes are cooked. Sprinkle with grated 'cheese' and serve with a salad.

Rice and vegetable pie (serves 4/6)

pastry

8oz/225g plain flour

1 rounded teaspoon baking powder

3 tablespoons olive oil

cold water

soya milk

sesame seeds

filling

6oz/175g ripe tomatoes, skinned and chopped

4oz/100g long grain rice

4oz/100g artichoke hearts, chopped

4oz/100g green pepper, chopped

1oz/25g vegan 'cheese', grated

1oz/25g black olives, chopped

1 onion, peeled and finely chopped

2 garlic cloves, crushed

1 tablespoon olive oil

1 tablespoon finely grated lemon peel

1 tablespoon lemon juice

1 dessertspoon tomato purée

1 teaspoon dried parsley

1 teaspoon dried mint

½ teaspoon dried dill

black pepper

Cook the rice, drain and rinse under cold running water. Drain well. Heat the oil for the filling and fry the onion, garlic, green pepper and lemon peel until soft. Add the tomatoes, lemon juice, tomato purée, parsley, mint and dill and season with black pepper. Raise the heat and simmer for 3 minutes, stirring frequently. Remove from the heat and stir in the cooked rice, artichoke hearts, 'cheese' and olives, mixing thoroughly.

Sift the flour and baking powder into a bowl and add the oil. Mix well, then gradually add enough cold water to bind. Knead the dough, then take two-thirds and roll it out on a floured board to line a greased 8 inch/20cm round loose-bottomed flan tin. Roll out the remaining dough to fit the top. Spoon the filling evenly into the pie case and cover it with the pastry lid. Press the edges of the pastry together to join and score a lattice design in the top with a sharp knife. Make a few slits in the pastry, brush it with soya milk and sprinkle with sesame seeds. Bake the pie in a preheated oven at 180°C/350°F/Gas mark 4 for 35-40 minutes until golden brown. Carefully remove it from the tin and cut into wedges. Serve with vegetable and salad accompaniments.

Briami (serves 4)

2lb/900g potatoes, peeled and sliced

8oz/225g courgette, halved lengthwise and sliced

4oz/100g red pepper, sliced

4oz/100g mushrooms, wiped and sliced

1 red onion, peeled and sliced

3 garlic cloves, crushed

3 tablespoons olive oil

2 tablespoons red wine

1 tablespoon lemon juice

14oz/400g tin chopped tomatoes

1 bay leaf

1 tablespoon finely chopped fresh rosemary

1 tablespoon finely chopped fresh thyme

1 teaspoon fennel seeds

black pepper

grated vegan 'cheese'

chopped black olives

Cook the potato slices for 5 minutes and drain. Heat one tablespoonful of oil in a saucepan and fry the onion and garlic for 5 minutes. Remove from the heat and add the chopped tomatoes, wine, lemon juice, bay leaf, rosemary, thyme and fennel seeds, season with black pepper and stir well. Layer the potatoes, courgette, red pepper and mushrooms with this tomato and onion sauce, drizzling each layer with some of the remaining oil, in a deep earthenware casserole dish. Cover and bake in a preheated oven at 180°C/350°F/Gas mark 4 for about 1 hour until the vegetables are tender. Sprinkle the 'cheese' and olives on top and serve with a grain dish and warm bread.

Linguine with spinach, cauliflower and chickpea sauce (serves 4)

8oz/225g linguine

1lb/450g fresh spinach

12oz/350g cauliflower, cut into small florets

8oz/225g cooked chickpeas

1 onion, peeled and finely chopped

1 tablespoon olive oil

1oz/25g sultanas

8 fl.oz/225ml vegetable stock

1 rounded tablespoon finely chopped fresh parsley

1 rounded tablespoon finely chopped fresh marjoram

black pepper

10 fl.oz/300ml soya milk

½ oz/15g cornflour

grated vegan 'cheese'

chopped walnuts

Wash the spinach and put it in a large pan with only the water that clings to the leaves. Cook gently until done, drain and squeeze out excess liquid and chop the spinach finely. Fry the onion in the oil in a large saucepan for 5 minutes. Add the cauliflower, sultanas, stock, parsley and marjoram. Season with black pepper and stir well. Bring to the boil, cover and simmer gently until the cauliflower is just cooked. Dissolve the cornflour in the soya milk and add to the pan, together with the spinach and chickpeas. Mix well and bring to the boil, stirring frequently. Continue stirring for a minute or two until the sauce thickens. Cook the linguine until just tender, drain and divide between 4 plates. Spoon the sauce on top and garnish with grated 'cheese' and chopped walnuts. Serve with warm bread and a green salad.

Lemon-flavoured lentil stew (serves 4)

12oz/350g potatoes, peeled and diced

8oz/225g broccoli, chopped

8oz/225g leek, trimmed and sliced

4oz/100g green lentils

1 onion, peeled and chopped

2 garlic cloves, crushed

14oz/400g tin chopped tomatoes

1 large lemon

1 tablespoon olive oil

1 rounded teaspoon cumin seeds

1 bay leaf

black pepper

2 tablespoons finely chopped fresh coriander

1 dessertspoon capers, chopped

Soak the lentils in boiling water for 1 hour, drain and bring to the boil in fresh water. Cover and simmer for 30 minutes, then strain the cooking liquid into a measuring jug and make up to 10 fl.oz/300ml with water if necessary. Cut the lemon in half and cut one of the halves into slices for garnish. Squeeze the juice and grate the peel from the other half. Heat the oil in a large pan and fry the leek, onion, garlic and grated lemon peel until softened. Add the cumin seeds, bay leaf, coriander, lemon juice, drained lentils, potatoes and measured cooking liquid. Season with black pepper and stir well. Bring to the boil, cover and simmer for 10 minutes, stirring occasionally. Add the broccoli and chopped tomatoes and combine well. Bring back to the boil, cover and simmer gently, stirring occasionally, for about 20 minutes until the vegetables are tender. Spoon the stew into a serving dish and sprinkle the capers over the top. Garnish with the lemon slices and serve with a rice dish, warm bread and a salad.

Stuffed aubergines (serves 4)

2 aubergines (each approx. 10oz/300g)

4oz/100g red pepper, chopped

4oz/100g green pepper, chopped

2oz/50g natural minced textured vegetable protein

½ oz/15g currants

1 onion, peeled and finely chopped

2 garlic cloves, crushed

4 tablespoons olive oil

14 fl.oz/400ml vegetable stock

1 rounded teaspoon dried oregano

black pepper

extra olive oil

sauce

8oz/225g ripe tomatoes, skinned and chopped

1 garlic clove, crushed

1 dessertspoon olive oil

1 dessertspoon tomato purée

1 dessertspoon lemon juice

1 teaspoon dried basil

black pepper

topping

grated vegan 'cheese'

toasted pine kernels

Cut the aubergines in half lengthwise and scoop out the flesh, leaving the shells about ¼ inch/5mm thick. Finely chop the flesh and fry it with the onion and garlic in the 4 tablespoonfuls of oil for 5 minutes. Add the red and green peppers, vegetable protein, currants, stock and oregano and season with black pepper. Stir well and bring to the boil. Cover and simmer, stirring occasionally, for 10 minutes, then uncover and simmer for 5 minutes more until the liquid has been absorbed.

Brush the aubergine shells inside and out with olive oil and arrange them in a baking dish. Fill each shell with some of the filling, then cover and bake in a preheated oven at 180°C/350°F/Gas mark 4 for about 45 minutes until done. Meanwhile, make the sauce. Fry the garlic in the oil and add the remaining sauce ingredients. Stir well and simmer for about 10 minutes, stirring occasionally, until the sauce thickens. Spoon the hot sauce over the cooked aubergines and garnish with grated 'cheese' and pine kernels. Serve with a grain dish and a salad.

Bulgar, vegetable and chickpea casserole (serves 4)

8oz/225g fresh spinach, chopped

8oz/225g leek, trimmed and sliced

8oz/225g shelled broad beans

8oz/225g cooked chickpeas

4oz/100g mushrooms, wiped and sliced

14oz/400g tin chopped tomatoes

6oz/175g bulgar wheat

2 garlic cloves, crushed

14 fl.oz/400ml vegetable stock

1 tablespoon olive oil

1 tablespoon red wine

1 dessertspoon red wine vinegar

1 dessertspoon tomato purée

1 rounded teaspoon dried dill

black pepper

grated vegan 'cheese

Heat the oil in a large pan and fry the leek and garlic for 5 minutes. Add the spinach, cover and cook for about 5 minutes until it wilts. Remove the saucepan from the heat and add the chickpeas, mushrooms, tomatoes, wine, vinegar, tomato purée and dill. Cook the broad beans, drain, rinse under cold water and slip them from their skins. Add the beans to the pan together with the bulgar wheat and stock. Season with black pepper and stir well. Transfer the mixture to a greased casserole dish, cover and bake in a preheated oven at 180°C/350°F/Gas mark 4 for 40 minutes. Sprinkle with grated 'cheese' and serve with warm bread and a salad.

Spanakopita (serves 4)

10oz/300g filo pastry

olive oil

sesame seeds

filling

1½lb/675g fresh spinach

8oz/225g vegan 'cream cheese'

2oz/50g vegan 'cheese', grated

1 onion, peeled and finely chopped

1 dessertspoon olive oil

1 teaspoon dried dill

black pepper

Wash the spinach leaves and cook them gently in a large saucepan with only the water that clings to them. Allow to cool slightly, then squeeze out as much water as possible and chop the spinach finely.

Fry the onion in the oil until soft, then remove from the heat and add the spinach and the remaining filling ingredients. Mix thoroughly until well combined.

Cut the sheets of filo pastry in half so that they measure about 10 x 9 inches/25 x 23cm. Put 3 sheets of filo on top of each other on a greased baking sheet, brushing between each sheet with olive oil. Spread a third of the filling evenly over the pastry, leaving a gap aground the edges for tucking in. Repeat these layers twice and finish with the remaining filo sheets, then tuck the pastry edges in. Brush the top with olive oil and sprinkle with sesame seeds. Bake in a preheated oven at 180°C/350°F/Gas mark 4 for 25-30 minutes until golden brown. Serve with vegetable accompaniments.

Baked macaroni (serves 4)

6oz/175g macaroni

4oz/100g red pepper, chopped

4oz/100g green pepper, chopped

2oz/50g mushrooms, wiped and chopped

2oz/50g natural minced textured vegetable protein

14oz/400g tin chopped tomatoes

12 fl.oz/350ml vegetable stock

1 red onion, peeled and chopped

2 garlic cloves, crushed

1 tablespoon olive oil

1 tablespoon tomato purée

1 bay leaf

1 rounded teaspoon dried thyme

black pepper

sauce

10 fl.oz/300ml soya milk

2oz/50g vegan 'cheese', grated

½ oz/15g cornflour

topping

1oz/25g breadcrumbs

1 rounded tablespoon vegan 'Parmesan'

Heat the oil in a large pan and fry the onion, garlic and red and green peppers for 5 minutes, then add the mushrooms, vegetable protein, stock, tomato purée, bay leaf and thyme and stir well. Bring to the boil, cover and simmer for 10 minutes, stirring occasionally. Remove from the heat and stir in the chopped tomatoes. Cook the macaroni until just tender, drain and add to the sauce, season with black pepper and combine thoroughly. Spoon the mixture into a greased baking dish.

Mix the cornflour with the soya milk until smooth, pour it into a saucepan and add the grated 'cheese'. Bring to the boil while stirring and continue stirring until the sauce thickens. Pour the sauce evenly over the macaroni mixture. Mix the breadcrumbs with the 'Parmesan' and sprinkle over the top. Cover the dish with foil and bake in a preheated oven at 180°C/350°F/Gas mark 4 for 25 minutes. Remove the foil and bake for a further 10 minutes until browned. Serve with a plain vegetable or salad.

Potato-topped rice and bean casserole (serves 4)

1¼lb/550g potatoes, peeled and thinly sliced

8oz/225g cooked haricot beans

4oz/100g long grain rice

14oz/400g tin chopped tomatoes

4oz/100g green pepper, chopped

1 onion, peeled and chopped

1 garlic clove, crushed

3 tablespoons water

1 tablespoon lemon juice

1 tablespoon olive oil

1 bay leaf

1 teaspoon dried mint

1 teaspoon dried dill

black pepper

extra olive oil

finely chopped fresh parsley

Cook the rice, drain, rinse under cold running water and drain well. Heat the tablespoonful of oil in a large saucepan and fry the onion, garlic and green pepper until soft. Remove from the heat and add the chopped tomatoes, rice, beans, water, lemon juice, bay leaf, mint and dill. Season with black pepper, mixing thoroughly, then transfer to a greased shallow baking dish. Boil the potato slices for 5 minutes, drain and arrange on top of the rice mixture. Brush the slices with olive oil and bake the casserole in a preheated oven at 180°C/350°F/Gas mark 4 for about 35 minutes until golden. Garnish with chopped parsley and serve with a plain vegetable or a green salad.

VEGETABLES

As well as being used as accompaniments for main courses, some of the following could be served with grain dishes and bread to make light meals. Other easily prepared and typical vegetable dishes include seasonally available produce such as asparagus, spinach, new potatoes, artichoke hearts, broad beans, courgettes, broccoli and cauliflower. These can be lightly steamed and given a Greek-style flavour by serving them with one of the sauces or dressings from pages 93-95.

Lemon and garlic roasted potatoes (serves 4)

2lb/900g potatoes, peeled

2 garlic cloves, crushed

1 tablespoon olive oil

1 tablespoon lemon juice

black pepper

lemon wedges

Cut the potatoes into even-sized chunks and boil them for 5 minutes. Mix the garlic with the oil and lemon juice and season with black pepper. Drain the potatoes and return to the pan, then add the oil mixture and toss well. Transfer to a baking dish and bake in a preheated oven at 180°C/350°F/Gas mark 4 for 35-40 minutes until golden brown. Serve garnished with lemon wedges.

Cauliflower and mushroom stifado (serves 4)

1lb/450g cauliflower, cut into small florets

4oz/100g mushrooms, wiped and chopped

1 onion, peeled and finely chopped

2 garlic cloves, crushed

6 fl.oz/175ml water

1 rounded tablespoon tomato purée

1 bay leaf

1 teaspoon paprika

1 teaspoon dried rosemary

black pepper

2 tablespoons olive oil

1 tablespoon red wine vinegar

finely chopped fresh parsley

Soften the onion and garlic in the oil in a large pan. Add the mushrooms and fry until the juices begin to run. Mix the tomato purée and paprika with the water until smooth, then add to the pan together with the cauliflower, bay leaf and rosemary. Season with black pepper and mix thoroughly. Bring to the boil and simmer uncovered for about 15 minutes, stirring occasionally, until the cauliflower is tender. Remove from the heat and stir in the vinegar. Spoon into a serving bowl and serve at room temperature, garnished with parsley.

Courgettes with peppers (serves 4)

12oz/350g courgettes, chopped

4oz/100g red pepper, chopped

4oz/100g yellow pepper, chopped

4oz/100g tomato, skinned and chopped

1 red onion, peeled and finely chopped

1 garlic clove, crushed

1 tablespoon olive oil

1 tablespoon red wine

1 dessertspoon tomato purée

1 dessertspoon balsamic vinegar

1 teaspoon coriander seeds, crushed

black pepper

Fry the red and yellow peppers, onion and garlic in the oil for 5 minutes. Add the courgette, tomato, red wine, tomato purée and coriander seeds and season with black pepper. Stir well, then simmer covered, stirring occasionally, for about 10 minutes until the courgette is just done. Remove from the heat and stir in the vinegar before serving.

Oven-braised potatoes with leeks (serves 4)

1lb/450g potatoes, peeled and thinly sliced

8oz/225g leek, trimmed and sliced

1 garlic clove, crushed

1 rounded tablespoon finely chopped fresh parsley

1 tablespoon olive oil

1 tablespoon lemon juice

5 fl.oz/150ml vegetable stock

black pepper

fresh parsley sprigs

Put the potatoes, leek, garlic, chopped parsley, oil and lemon juice in a casserole dish and mix well. Season with black pepper and pour the vegetable stock over the top. Cover tightly with foil and bake in a preheated oven at 200°C/400°F/Gas mark 6 for 35-40 minutes until cooked. Garnish with fresh parsley sprigs when serving.

Okra in tomato sauce (serves 4)

12oz/350g okra

8oz/225g ripe tomatoes, skinned and finely chopped

1 onion, peeled and finely chopped

2 garlic cloves, crushed

2 tablespoons olive oil

1 tablespoon balsamic vinegar

1 tablespoon lemon juice

5 fl.oz/150ml water

1 dessertspoon tomato purée

1 bay leaf

2 tablespoons finely chopped fresh parsley

black pepper

fresh parsley sprigs

Cut the stalks from the okra and discard. Fry the whole okra with the onion and garlic in the oil for 5 minutes. Add the remaining ingredients, except the parsley sprigs, and stir well. Bring to the boil, then cover and simmer gently, stirring regularly, until the okra is tender. Transfer to a serving dish and serve either warm or cold, garnished with fresh parsley sprigs.

Potato and olive stew (serves 4)

1½lb/675g potatoes, peeled and diced

4oz/100g tomato, skinned and finely chopped

2oz/50g black olives, chopped

1 onion, peeled and finely chopped

1 garlic clove, crushed

1 tablespoon olive oil

1 tablespoon lemon juice

2 tablespoons water

1 dessertspoon tomato purée

1 rounded teaspoon dried oregano

black pepper

finely chopped fresh parsley

Fry the onion and garlic in the oil in a large pan for 5 minutes. Dissolve the tomato purée in the water and add, together with the remaining ingredients apart from the olives and parsley. Bring to the boil, cover and simmer gently, stirring regularly, for about 20 minutes until the potatoes are done, adding a little more water if necessary to prevent sticking. Stir in the olives and serve garnished with fresh parsley.

Baked beetroot (serves 4)

1lb/450g beetroot, peeled and grated

1oz/25g raisins

1 garlic clove, crushed

2 tablespoons red wine vinegar

2 tablespoons fresh orange juice

1 tablespoon olive oil

black pepper

Put all the ingredients in a large bowl and mix thoroughly. Transfer to a greased casserole dish and cover tightly with foil. Bake in a preheated oven at 180°C/350°F/Gas mark 4 for 1 hour. Stir the beetroot before serving at room temperature.

Marinated roasted vegetables (serves 4)

6oz/175g aubergine, diced

6oz/175g courgette, sliced

4oz/100g tomato, cut into wedges

4oz/100g red pepper, sliced

2oz/50g mushrooms, wiped and sliced

1 medium red onion, peeled and sliced

2 garlic cloves, crushed

3 tablespoons olive oil

1 tablespoon lemon juice

1 dessertspoon balsamic vinegar

1 teaspoon dried rosemary

1 teaspoon dried thyme

black pepper

1 bay leaf

finely chopped fresh parsley

Put the aubergine, courgette, tomato, red pepper, mushrooms and onion in a bowl. Mix the olive oil with the lemon juice, vinegar, rosemary, thyme and garlic and spoon over the vegetables, then add the bay leaf and season with black pepper. Combine well, cover and refrigerate for 4 hours. Stir the mixture again and transfer it to a shallow casserole dish. Cover with foil and bake in a preheated oven at 180°C/350°F/Gas mark 4 for about 50 minutes until cooked. Garnish with chopped parsley to serve.

Orzo with leek and tomato sauce (serves 4)

8oz/225g leek, trimmed and sliced

4oz/100g orzo

14oz/400g tin chopped tomatoes

1 garlic clove, crushed

1 tablespoon olive oil

1 tablespoon red wine

1 tablespoon lemon juice

1 dessertspoon tomato purée

1 teaspoon coriander seeds, crushed

½ teaspoon dried thyme

black pepper

grated vegan 'cheese'

Fry the leek and garlic in the oil for 10 minutes in a large pan, stirring occasionally. Add the chopped tomatoes, wine, tomato purée, coriander and thyme and season with black pepper, stir well and bring to the boil. Cover and simmer, stirring occasionally, for 10 minutes. Meanwhile cook the orzo until just tender, then drain and add to the sauce. Mix thoroughly, then spoon into a serving dish and garnish with grated 'cheese'.

Minted potato croquettes (makes 12)

2lb/900g potatoes, peeled

2 tablespoons olive oil

1 rounded tablespoon vegan 'Parmesan'

1 dessertspoon dried mint, crumbled

black pepper

sesame seeds

extra olive oil

Cut the potatoes into even-sized chunks and boil them. Drain and dry off over a low heat, then mash with the 2 tablespoonfuls of oil. Stir in the 'Parmesan' and mint and season with black pepper. Allow to cool slightly, then take rounded tablespoonfuls and shape into croquettes. Roll each croquette in sesame seeds until it is completely covered. Put them on a plate, cover and chill for 2 hours. Brush the croquettes all over with olive oil and bake them in a preheated oven at 180°C/350°F/Gas mark 4 for 25-30 minutes until golden brown.

Green vegetables with chickpeas (serves 4)

8oz/225g fresh spinach, shredded

4oz/100g green beans, topped, tailed and chopped

4oz/100g broccoli, chopped

4oz/100g cooked chickpeas

½oz/15g sultanas

1 onion, peeled and finely chopped

1 garlic clove, crushed

1 dessertspoon olive oil

4 fl.oz/125ml water

½ teaspoon dried dill

black pepper

5 fl.oz/150ml soya milk

1 rounded dessertspoon cornflour

chopped walnuts

Heat the oil in a large saucepan and fry the onion and garlic for 5 minutes. Add the spinach and cook gently until it wilts. Stir in the green beans, broccoli, sultanas, water and dill and season with black pepper. Bring to the boil, cover and simmer for about 15 minutes, stirring occasionally, until the vegetables are tender. Dissolve the cornflour in the soya milk and add to the pan with the chickpeas. Bring to the boil while stirring and continue stirring for a minute or two until the mixture thickens. Serve garnished with chopped walnuts.

Mixed beans in tomato sauce (serves 4)

8oz/225g cooked mixed beans

8oz/225g ripe tomatoes, skinned and chopped

4oz/100g green beans, topped, tailed and chopped

1 red onion, peeled and finely chopped

1 garlic clove, crushed

1 dessertspoon olive oil

1 dessertspoon tomato purée

2 tablespoons water

1 teaspoon dried oregano

½ teaspoon paprika

black pepper

1 dessertspoon balsamic vinegar

chopped fresh parsley

Soften the onion and garlic in the oil. Add the green beans and water and simmer for 3 minutes, then stir in the tomatoes, tomato purée, oregano and paprika and season with black pepper. Simmer covered for 10 minutes, stirring occasionally. Add the cooked beans and continue simmering for a minute or two. Remove from the heat and stir in the vinegar. Spoon into a serving dish and garnish with parsley.

GRAIN ACCOMPANIMENTS

Barley, rice and wheat are all commonly used grains and these can be either plainly served or made into more elaborate dishes with the addition of other ingredients. They are often used as accompaniments for main courses, especially stews and casseroles, but they can also be turned into light meals themselves when served with bread and salads. Soups and many of the mezedes can be made into main courses by serving them with a grain dish. Highly nutritious and infinitely versatile, these easy-to-prepare grain dishes taste equally good served warm or cold.

Mixed grains with beans (serves 4)

6oz/175g cooked cannellini beans

2oz/50g pot barley

20z/50g wheat berries

2oz/50g bulgar wheat

1 onion, peeled and finely chopped

1 garlic clove, crushed

½oz/15g currants

1 dessertspoon olive oil

1 tablespoon lemon juice

1 teaspoon cumin seeds

1 teaspoon dried mint

black pepper

fresh mint leaves

Soak the barley and wheat berries in boiling water for 2 hours. Drain and bring to the boil in a fresh pan of water. Cover and simmer for 30 minutes, then strain the cooking liquid into a measuring jug and make up to 15 fl.oz/450ml with water, if necessary.

Fry the onion and garlic in the oil in a large pan for 5 minutes. Add the cumin seeds and stir around for 30 seconds, then the barley and wheat berries, bulgar, beans, currants and mint and the measured liquid. Season with black pepper and stir well. Bring to the boil, cover and simmer gently until the liquid has been absorbed. Remove from the heat, stir in the lemon juice and serve garnished with fresh mint leaves.

Tomato and artichoke rice (serves 4)

8oz/225g long grain brown rice

8oz/225g ripe tomatoes, skinned and finely chopped

8oz/225g artichoke hearts, chopped

1 tablespoon olive oil

1 garlic clove, crushed

1 dessertspoon tomato purée

1 tablespoon finely chopped fresh basil

1 tablespoon finely chopped fresh oregano

1 bay leaf

black pepper

20 fl.oz/600ml vegetable stock

grated vegan 'cheese'

chopped black olives

Fry the rice and garlic in the oil for 2 minutes. Add the remaining ingredients, except the 'cheese' and olives, and stir well. Bring to the boil, cover and simmer gently until the liquid has been absorbed. Transfer to a serving bowl and garnish with grated 'cheese' and olives.

Minted bulgar with leeks (serves 4)

1lb/450g leeks, trimmed and finely sliced

8oz/225g bulgar wheat

1 tablespoon olive oil

1 garlic clove, crushed

20 fl.oz/600ml vegetable stock

1 dessertspoon dried mint

1 bay leaf

black pepper

fresh mint leaves

Soften the leeks and garlic in the oil for 10 minutes. Add the bulgar wheat, stock, dried mint and bay leaf and season with black pepper. Stir well and bring to the boil, then cover and simmer gently until the liquid has been absorbed and the wheat is done. Garnish with fresh mint leaves when serving.

Spiced bean pilaff (serves 4)

8oz/225g long grain brown rice

8oz/225g cooked mixed beans (e.g. butter, haricot, flageolet)

8oz/225g green beans, topped, tailed and cut into ½ inch/1cm
   lengths

1oz/25g sultanas

1 onion, peeled and finely chopped

2 garlic cloves, crushed

1 tablespoon olive oil

22 fl.oz/650ml vegetable stock

1 teaspoon coriander seeds, crushed

1 teaspoon cumin seeds

6 cloves

1 inch/2.5cm stick of cinnamon

4 cardamom pods, husked and the seeds separated

black pepper

chopped fresh coriander leaves

Fry the onion and garlic in the oil for 5 minutes in a large saucepan. Add the rice and spices and stir around for 30 seconds, then stir in the remaining ingredients apart from the fresh coriander. Bring to the boil, cover and simmer gently until the liquid has been absorbed. Spoon into a serving dish and garnish with chopped coriander.

Spinach rice (serves 4)

1lb/450g fresh spinach, finely chopped

8oz/225g long grain rice

1 onion, peeled and finely chopped

1 tablespoon olive oil

1 tablespoon lemon juice

1 tablespoon finely chopped fresh dill

20 fl.oz/600ml water

black pepper

plain soya yoghurt

lemon wedges

Heat the oil in a large pan and fry the onion until softened. Add the spinach and cook gently until it wilts. Stir in the rice, lemon juice, dill and water and season with black pepper, then bring to the boil, cover and simmer gently until the liquid has been absorbed. Transfer to a warmed serving dish and swirl a little yoghurt on top. Garnish with lemon wedges.

Saffron and sweet pepper rice (serves 4)

8oz/225g long grain rice

8oz/225g mixed peppers, finely chopped

1 onion, peeled and finely chopped

1 tablespoon olive oil

a few saffron threads

black pepper

20 fl.oz/600ml vegetable stock

pepper rings

Fry the onion and chopped peppers in the oil until soft. Add the rice and stir around for 30 seconds, then stir in the stock and saffron and season with black pepper. Bring to the boil, cover and simmer gently until the liquid has been absorbed. Garnish with pepper rings to serve.

Mushroom pilaff (serves 4)

8oz/225g long grain brown rice

8oz/225g mushrooms, wiped and chopped

1 onion, peeled and finely chopped

2 garlic cloves, crushed

1 tablespoon olive oil

2 tablespoons finely chopped fresh parsley

1 spring of fresh thyme

18 fl.oz/550ml vegetable stock

2 fl.oz/50ml white wine

black pepper

1 tablespoon lemon juice

fresh parsley sprigs

Heat the oil in a large saucepan and soften the onion and garlic. Add the rice and stir around for 1 minute, then the mushrooms, chopped parsley, thyme, stock and wine. Season with black pepper, bring to the boil, cover and simmer gently until the liquid has been absorbed. Remove from the heat and stir in the lemon juice. Spoon into a dish and garnish with fresh parsley sprigs.

Chickpea and lemon rice (serves 4)

8oz/225g long grain rice

8oz/225g cooked chickpeas

1 onion, peeled and finely chopped

1 lemon

2 tablespoons olive oil

18 fl.oz/550ml vegetable stock

black pepper

chopped walnuts

Cut the lemon in half and cut one of the halves into slices for garnish. Squeeze the juice from the other half and finely grate the peel. Heat 1 tablespoonful of oil in a large pan and fry the onion and grated lemon peel until soft. Add the rice and move it around for 30 seconds. Stir in the stock and chickpeas and season with black pepper. Bring to the boil, cover and simmer gently until the liquid has been absorbed. Combine the lemon juice with the remaining oil and add to the rice. Mix thoroughly, then spoon the rice into a serving dish and sprinkle it with chopped walnuts. Garnish with the lemon slices.

SALADS

As well as the more usual salad ingredients, Greeks are fond of using wild green leaves, khorta, to make interesting green salads. These leaves are combined with freshly picked herbs and lightly dressed with an olive oil and lemon dressing. Other favourite ingredients include beans and lentils, pasta and grains. Salads are served as accompaniments to main courses or as mezedes. They are also used to fill pitta breads and served as a snack.

Potato and sun-dried tomato salad (serves 4)

2lb/900g potatoes, peeled

½oz/15g sun-dried tomatoes, finely chopped

6 tablespoons water

2 dessertspoons olive oil

1 dessertspoon lemon juice

1 dessertspoon balsamic vinegar

1 garlic clove, crushed

½ teaspoon dried oregano

black pepper

quartered cherry tomatoes

chopped fresh parsley

Put the sun-dried tomatoes and water in a small pan and bring to the boil. Cover and simmer until the liquid has been absorbed. Remove from the heat and add the olive oil, lemon juice, vinegar, garlic and oregano, season with black pepper and mix thoroughly. Cut the potatoes into even-sized chunks and boil them. Drain and dice the potatoes, then add the dressing. Toss well and serve either warm or cold, garnished with cherry tomatoes and parsley.

Roasted pepper and rice salad (serves 4)

12oz/350g mixed peppers

4oz/100g long grain rice

2oz/50g cucumber, chopped

1 small red onion, peeled

6 black olives, chopped

finely chopped fresh parsley

dressing

1 tablespoon olive oil

1 dessertspoon lemon juice

1 teaspoon dried oregano

1 garlic clove, crushed

black pepper

Put the peppers on a baking tray and grill them, turning occasionally, until the skins blister. Allow to cool slightly, then carefully remove the skins, stalks, membranes and seeds and chop the flesh. Put this in a mixing bowl with the olives and cucumber. Cook the rice, drain and rinse under cold running water. Drain well and add to the bowl. Cut a few rings from the onion for garnish, finely chop the rest and add to the salad. Mix the dressing ingredients, pour over the salad and toss thoroughly. Garnish with chopped parsley and the onion rings.

Chickpea salad (serves 4)

8oz/225g cooked chickpeas

8oz/225g mixed peppers, finely chopped

4oz/100g tomato, skinned and finely chopped

3oz/75g cucumber, finely chopped

1 small red onion, peeled and finely chopped

8 black olives, chopped

1 garlic clove, crushed

2 dessertspoons olive oil

1 dessertspoon balsamic vinegar

1 tablespoon finely chopped fresh thyme

black pepper

fresh thyme sprigs

Mix the chickpeas, peppers, cucumber, onion and olives in a large bowl. Combine the tomato with the garlic, olive oil, vinegar and chopped thyme, season with black pepper and add to the salad. Toss very well and transfer to a serving bowl. Serve garnished with sprigs of fresh thyme.

Pasta salad (serves 4/6)

4oz/100g pasta spirals

4oz/100g cherry tomatoes, halved

4oz/100g red pepper, chopped

4oz/100g yellow pepper, chopped

4oz/100g cooked chickpeas

2oz/50g green seedless grapes, halved

2oz/50g cucumber, chopped

2oz/50g black olives, chopped

2oz/50g vegan 'cheese', diced

2 tablespoons olive oil

1 dessertspoon balsamic vinegar

1 dessertspoon lemon juice

1 teaspoon dried oregano

1 garlic clove, crushed

black pepper

chopped fresh parsley

Cook the pasta, drain and rinse under cold running water. Drain well and put it in a bowl with the tomatoes, peppers, grapes, chickpeas, cucumber, olives and 'cheese'. Mix the olive oil with the vinegar, lemon juice, oregano and garlic and season with black pepper. Add to the salad and toss well. Garnish with fresh parsley when serving.

Avocado and fruit salad (serves 4)

1 large avocado, peeled, stoned and diced

1 orange

1 apple, peeled, cored and diced

10 black seedless grapes, halved

4oz/100g red pepper, chopped

4oz/100g tomato, chopped

1oz/25g walnuts, chopped

½ bunch of watercress, trimmed and chopped

lemon juice

1 dessertspoon olive oil

½ teaspoon coriander seed, crushed

black pepper

Peel the orange, remove the pith, membranes and pips and chop the segments. Strain the juice into a small bowl and mix with the oil. Sprinkle the avocado and apple with lemon juice and put in a mixing bowl with the chopped orange, grapes, red pepper, tomato, walnuts, watercress and crushed coriander seeds. Add the orange dressing and season with black pepper. Toss thoroughly, then transfer to a serving bowl.

Warm green salad (serves 4)

This salad is traditionally made with the green leafy tops of turnip, beetroot and radish as well as dandelion and purslane leaves.

12oz/350g mixed green leaves

2 tablespoons olive oil

1 dessertspoon white wine vinegar

1 teaspoon lemon juice

½ teaspoon mild mustard

1 garlic clove, crushed

black pepper

finely sliced spring onions

Mix the oil with the vinegar, lemon juice, mustard and garlic. Steam the leaves until just tender, then add the dressing and season with black pepper. Toss very well, spoon into a serving bowl and garnish with spring onions.

Green lentil and olive salad (serves 4)

4oz/100g green lentils

2oz/50g green olives, chopped

2oz/50g cucumber, finely chopped

1 rounded tablespoon capers, chopped

4 spring onions, trimmed and finely sliced

1 garlic clove, crushed

2 tablespoons finely chopped fresh parsley

1 tablespoon olive oil

1 dessertspoon lemon juice

black pepper

Cook the lentils, drain and put them in a mixing bowl with the olives, cucumber, capers, onions and parsley. Mix the olive oil with the lemon juice and garlic and add to the salad, season with black pepper and toss. Transfer to a serving bowl and serve at room temperature.

Pea and orzo salad (serves 4)

4oz/100g orzo

4oz/100g shelled peas

2oz/50g red pepper, finely chopped

2oz/50g tomato, skinned and finely chopped

1oz/25g cucumber, finely chopped

1oz/25g black olives, finely chopped

4 spring onions, trimmed and finely sliced

1 garlic clove, crushed

1 tablespoon olive oil

1dessertspoon red wine vinegar

1 tablespoon finely chopped fresh dill

black pepper

grated vegan 'cheese'

Cook the pasta until just tender, then drain and rinse under cold running water. Drain well and place in a large bowl. Cook the peas, drain and add to the pasta together with the red pepper, tomato, cucumber, olives, spring onions and dill. Mix the oil with the vinegar and garlic and pour over the salad. Season with black pepper and toss thoroughly. Spoon into a serving bowl and ganish with grated 'cheese'.

Bulgar, bean and walnut salad (serves 4)

4oz/100g bulgar wheat
4oz/100g cooked cannellini beans
1oz/25g walnuts, chopped
1 medium red onion, peeled and finely chopped
1 medium tomato, skinned and finely chopped
8 fl.oz/225ml boiling water
1 dessertspoon tomato purée
2 dessertspoons olive oil
1 dessertspoon lemon juice
½ teaspoon ground cumin
½ teaspoon ground coriander
½ teaspoon paprika
black pepper
shredded lettuce
finely chopped fresh coriander leaves

Dissolve the tomato purée in the water and add the bulgar wheat. Cover and leave to soak for 30 minutes. Heat 1 dessertspoonful of oil in a pan and fry the onion until soft. Add the cumin, coriander and paprika, stir around for a few seconds and remove from the heat. Put the bulgar in a sieve and press out any excess liquid with the back of a spoon, then add it to the onion together with the beans, walnuts and tomato. Mix the remaining oil with the lemon juice and add to the salad, season with black pepper and mix well. Arrange some shredded lettuce on a serving plate and spoon the salad on top. Garnish with chopped coriander.

Marinated pepper and mushroom salad (serves 4)

1lb/450g mixed peppers

8oz/225g mushrooms, wiped and sliced

4 spring onions, trimmed and finely sliced

2 garlic cloves, crushed

2 tablespoons olive oil

2 tablespoons white wine

1 tablespoon lemon juice

1 teaspoon fennel seeds, crushed

1 teaspoon dried thyme

1 bay leaf

black pepper

chopped black olives

fresh fennel leaves

Place the peppers under a hot grill, turning occasionally, until the skins blister. Allow to cool slightly, then carefully remove the skins, stalks, membranes and seeds. Chop the peppers and put them in a large bowl with the mushrooms and spring onions. Mix the olive oil with the garlic, wine, lemon juice, fennel seeds and thyme and add to the vegetables together with the bay leaf. Season with black pepper and mix thoroughly. Transfer to a serving bowl, cover and refrigerate overnight. Remove the bay leaf and garnish the salad with chopped olives and fennel leaves when serving.

Horiatiki (serves 4/6)

8oz/225g tomatoes, cut into wedges

4oz/100g cucumber, chopped

4oz/100g red pepper, chopped

4oz/100g yellow pepper, chopped

4oz/100g vegan 'cheese', diced

½ small red onion, peeled and sliced

1oz/25g black olives, halved

1 dessertspoon capers

1 dessertspoon finely chopped fresh dill

1 dessertspoon finely chopped fresh oregano

black pepper

2 tablespoons olive oil

2 dessertspoons lemon juice

shredded crisp lettuce leaves

Put the tomatoes, cucumber, red and yellow peppers, 'cheese', onion, olives and capers in a bowl and mix. Combine the herbs with the olive oil and lemon juice and season with black pepper. Spoon this dressing over the salad and toss well. Arrange some shredded lettuce leaves on a serving plate and pile the salad on top.

Spinach and tomato salad (serves 4)

4oz/100g fresh tender spinach, shredded

4oz/100g cherry tomatoes, quartered

4 spring onions, trimmed and finely sliced

1 garlic clove, crushed

1 tablespoon olive oil

1 dessertspoon lemon juice

1 teaspoon white wine vinegar

pinch of ground cinnamon

black pepper

chopped walnuts

Put the spinach, tomatoes and spring onions in a large bowl. Mix the garlic with the olive oil, lemon juice, vinegar and cinnamon, season with black pepper and add to the salad. Toss thoroughly, then spoon into a serving bowl and garnish with chopped walnuts.

Courgette and broad bean salad (serves 4/6)

1lb/450g courgettes

1lb/450g shelled broad beans

2 garlic cloves, crushed

1 tablespoon olive oil

1 teaspoon dried dill

1 teaspoon dried mint

1 dessertspoon lemon juice

black pepper

4 rounded tablespoons plain soya yoghurt

fresh mint leaves

Steam the broad beans until tender, rinse under cold running water and slip the beans from their skins. Cut the courgettes in half lengthwise, then into diagonal slices. Fry the courgette and garlic in the oil until just done. Add the skinned beans, dill, mint and lemon juice and season with black pepper. Stir around for a minute or two, then remove from the heat and stir in the yoghurt. Mix well, transfer to a serving dish and garnish with fresh mint leaves. Serve either at room temperature or chilled.

Fennel and avocado salad (serves 4)

8oz/225g fennel

2 medium avocados, peeled, stoned and diced

4oz/100g tomato, skinned and finely chopped

1 garlic clove, crushed

1/2 teaspoon dried thyme

black pepper

2 dessertspoons olive oil

1 dessertspoon lemon juice

trimmed watercress leaves

chopped fresh fennel leaves

Cut the fennel first into 1 inch/2.5cm lengths, then into thin strips and steam them for a few minutes to soften. Rinse under cold water to refresh, drain well and put in a mixing bowl with the avocado and tomato. Mix the garlic with the thyme, olive oil and lemon juice and spoon over the salad, season with black pepper and toss well. Arrange some watercress leaves on a serving plate, pile the salad on top and garnish with chopped fennel leaves.

Herby bean and artichoke salad (serves 4)

8oz/225g artichoke hearts, chopped

4oz/100g shelled broad beans

4oz/100g mixed cooked beans

4oz/100g green beans, topped, tailed and cut into ½ inch/1 cm lengths

2oz/50g fennel, finely chopped

4 spring onions, trimmed and sliced

2 rounded tablespoons finely chopped fresh herbs (e.g. oregano, thyme, rosemary)

1 garlic clove, crushed

1 tablespoon olive oil

1 teaspoon lemon juice

black pepper

fresh fennel leaves

Steam the broad beans, rinse under cold running water and slip them from the skins. Put the beans in a bowl with the artichokes, mixed cooked beans, fennel, spring onions and herbs. Steam the green beans until just tender, rinse under cold water and add to the salad. Combine the garlic with the olive oil and lemon juice and add to the salad. Season with black pepper and toss thoroughly. Spoon into a serving bowl, cover and put in the fridge until cold. Serve garnished with fresh fennel leaves.

Courgette and mushroom salad (serves 4/6)

1lb/450g courgette, chopped

8oz/225g mushrooms, wiped and chopped

4oz/100g tomato, skinned and finely chopped

1 garlic clove, crushed

4 spring onions, trimmed and finely sliced

1 tablespoon olive oil

1 dessertspoon balsamic vinegar

1 teaspoon coriander seeds, crushed

1 teaspoon dried thyme

black pepper

finely chopped fresh parsley

Heat the oil and fry the mushrooms and garlic for 2 minutes. Steam the courgette for a few minutes to soften slightly, then add to the mushrooms together with the tomato, spring onions, vinegar, coriander seeds and thyme. Season with black pepper and mix well. Transfer to a serving dish and garnish with parsley. Serve at room temperature or refrigerate until cold.

SAUCES AND DRESSINGS

Greek-style sauces and dressings are very easy to prepare and add an instant authentic flavour to plainly cooked vegetables or salad ingredients. Tsatsiki is probably the country's most famous dressing and this is served with virtually all types of food. It is especially good spooned over boiled new potatoes or steamed green vegetables and it can also be served as a dip.

Sun-dried tomato sauce (serves 4)

14oz/400g tin chopped tomatoes

1 red onion, peeled and finely chopped

1 garlic clove, crushed

1/2oz/15g sun-dried tomatoes, finely chopped

1 tablespoon olive oil

4 fl.oz/125ml water

1 teaspoon dried oregano

1 bay leaf

black pepper

1 dessertspoon balsamic vinegar

Fry the onion and garlic in the oil for 5 minutes. Add the sun-dried tomatoes and water and bring to the boil. Cover and simmer for 15 minutes, stirring occasionally, then add the tinned tomatoes, oregano and bay leaf and season with black pepper. Stir well, bring back to the boil, cover and simmer, stirring occasionally, for 15 minutes. Remove from the heat and stir in the vinegar before serving hot.

Tsatsiki (serves 4)

6 fl.oz/175ml plain soya yoghurt

4oz/100g cucumber, finely chopped

1 garlic clove, crushed

3 tablespoons finely chopped fresh mint

black pepper

Mix the ingredients well and serve chilled.

Skorthalia (serves 4)

2oz/50g ground almonds

2oz/50g white bread

4 fl.oz/125ml water

2 tablespoons lemon juice

2 tablespoons white wine vinegar

1 tablespoon olive oil

4 garlic cloves, chopped

black pepper

Soak the bread in the water for 30 minutes, then put it in a blender with the remaining ingredients and blend smooth.

Walnut and lemon sauce (serves 4)

2oz/50g walnuts, chopped

1oz/25g white bread

finely grated peel and juice of 1 lemon

1 garlic clove, chopped

2 tablespoons olive oil

4 rounded tablespoons
    plain soya yoghurt

black pepper

Blend the ingredients until smooth.

Tahini and parsley dressing (serves 4)

4 tablespoons light tahini

4 tablespoons finely chopped fresh parsley

4 tablespoons water

2 tablespoons lemon juice

1 garlic clove, crushed

black pepper

Mix all the ingredients until well combined.

Olive and yoghurt dressing (serves 4)

2oz/50g green olives, chopped

4 rounded tablespoons plain soya yoghurt

1 tablespoon lemon juice

black pepper

Blend all of the ingredients together until smooth.

Oregano and lemon dressing

4 rounded tablespoons finely chopped fresh oregano

6 tablespoons olive oil

2 tablespoons lemon juice

1 tablespoon white wine vinegar

1 tablespoon finely grated lemon peel

black pepper

Combine the ingredients well.

BREADS

Sweet and savoury breads form an important part of the Greek diet and some type of bread is eaten with every meal. To commemorate festivals and religious celebrations speciality breads are baked, for example St. Basil's bread, to which traditionally a small coin is added which it is believed will bring the finder luck. All breads are best eaten fresh on the day of baking, although they can be cut into slices, wrapped in foil and frozen.

Sun-dried tomato and onion bread

1lb/450g plain flour

½oz/15g sun-dried tomatoes, finely chopped

1 small red onion, peeled and grated

9 fl.oz/250ml water

½ sachet easy-blend yeast

½ teaspoon salt

1 rounded dessertspoon dried oregano

2 tablespoons olive oil

extra olive oil

black onion seeds

Bring the sun-dried tomatoes and water to the boil, simmer covered for 5 minutes, then transfer to a jug and leave for 15 minutes.

Combine the flour, yeast, salt and oregano in a large bowl. Stir in the onion and 2 tablespoonfuls of oil, then add the cooled tomatoes and liquid and mix until a soft dough forms. Knead the dough well, return it to the bowl, cover and leave in a warm place for 1 hour to rise. Knead the dough again, then shape it into a slightly flattened 6 inch/15cm circle. Transfer to a greased baking sheet and leave in a warm place for 30 minutes until risen. Brush the dough with olive oil and sprinkle it with onion seeds, then bake it in a preheated oven at 200°C/400°F/Gas mark 6 for about 25 minutes until golden brown and hollow sounding when tapped underneath. Cool on a wire rack before cutting.

Minted 'cheese' flatbread

8oz/225g plain flour

1½oz/40g vegan 'cheese', grated

½ sachet easy-blend yeast

pinch of salt

1 tablespoon olive oil

1 rounded dessertspoon dried mint, crumbled

approx. 4 fl.oz/125ml warm water

extra olive oil

Put the flour, yeast, salt and mint into a mixing bowl and combine. Add the tablespoonful of oil and mix well, then stir in the grated 'cheese'. Gradually add the water until a soft dough forms. Knead the dough well, then shape or roll it into a circle 7 inches/18cm in diameter. Transfer to a greased baking sheet and leave in a warm place for 1 hour until risen. Brush the top with olive oil, then bake in a preheated oven at 200°C/400°F/Gas mark 6 for about 15 minutes until golden. Allow to cool slightly before cutting into wedges.

Sesame bread

6oz/175g plain flour

6oz/175g plain wholemeal flour

½ sachet easy-blend yeast

½ teaspoon salt

2 tablespoons olive oil

1 rounded dessertspoon light tahini

approx. 6 fl.oz/175ml warm water

sesame seeds

Mix the two flours with the salt and yeast, add the olive oil and combine well. Dissolve the tahini in the warm water and gradually add to the bowl until a soft dough forms. Knead this well, then return it to the bowl. Cover and leave to rise for 1 hour in a warm place. Knead the dough again, shape it into a ball and roll this in sesame seeds until covered all over. Put the ball on a greased baking sheet and flatten it slightly into a 5 inch/13cm round. Leave in a warm place for 30 minutes to rise again. Mark a circle on top of the dough about 1 inch/2.5cm from the edge with a sharp knife. Bake in a preheated oven at 200°C/400°F/Gas mark 6 for 20-25 minutes until browned and hollow sounding when tapped underneath. Allow to cool on a wire rack.

Olive and oregano rolls (makes 6)

6oz/175g plain flour

6oz/175g plain wholemeal flour

2oz/50g olives, chopped

½ sachet easy-blend yeast

½ teaspoon salt

2 tablespoons olive oil

1 rounded dessertspoon dried oregano

approx. 7 fl.oz/200ml warm water

extra olive oil

Put the two flours, yeast, salt and oregano in a mixing bowl, add the olive oil and mix well. Stir in the olives, then gradually add the water until a soft dough forms. Knead the dough, return it to the bowl, cover and put in a warm place for 1 hour to rise. Knead the dough again and divide it into 6 equal pieces. Knead each piece of dough and shape it into a ball. Arrange 5 of the balls in a circle on a greased baking sheet and put the remaining one in the middle. Squeeze the dough together slightly to join, then leave to rise in a warm place for 30 minutes. Brush the rolls with olive oil and bake them in a preheated oven at 200°C/400°F/Gas mark 6 for about 20 minutes until golden brown. Turn out onto a wire rack and allow to cool before dividing into the separate rolls.

Mixed seed bread

6oz/175g plain flour

6oz/175g plain wholemeal flour

1oz/25g sesame seeds

1 tablespoon olive oil

½ sachet easy-blend yeast

½ teaspoon salt

1 rounded teaspoon aniseed, crushed

1 rounded teaspoon black onion seeds, crushed

approx. 7 fl.oz/200ml warm water

extra olive oil

extra aniseed and sesame and black onion seeds

Combine the two flours, sesame seeds, yeast, salt and crushed seeds in a large bowl, stir in the tablespoonful of oil and mix well. Gradually add the water until a soft dough forms. Knead the dough well, then return to the bowl, cover and leave in a warm place to rise for 45 minutes. Knead the dough again and shape it into an oval of about 7 inches/18cm long. Put this on a greased baking sheet and make 5 widthways slits in the top of the loaf. Again leave in a warm place for 45 minutes to rise, then cut through the slits again, brush the dough with olive oil and sprinkle it with a mixture of aniseed and sesame and black onion seeds. Bake in a preheated oven at 200°C/400°F/Gas mark 6 for 18-20 minutes until browned. Cool on a wire rack before cutting into slices.

Olive and 'cheese' bread

1lb/450g plain flour

½ sachet easy-blend yeast

½ teaspoon salt

1 rounded tablespoon dried rosemary

2 tablespoons olive oil

approx. 10 fl.oz/300ml warm water

2oz/50g green olives, chopped

1oz/25g vegan 'cheese', grated

extra olive oil

extra dried rosemary

Mix the flour, yeast, salt and tablespoonful of rosemary in a large bowl. Add the 2 tablespoonfuls of oil and stir well, then gradually add the water until a soft dough forms. Knead the dough thoroughly, return it to the bowl, cover and leave in a warm place for 1 hour to rise, then knead it again. Roll or shape it into an oblong of 10 x 8 inches/25 x 20cm, scatter the olives and 'cheese' over the dough and roll it up to enclose the filling. Form the roll into a ring and squeeze the edges together to join. Transfer to a greased baking sheet and leave in a warm place for 30 minutes to rise again. Brush the top with olive oil and sprinkle with rosemary, then bake in a preheated oven at 200°C/400°F/Gas mark 6 for 20-25 minutes until golden. Allow to cool on a wire rack.

Christmas bread

8oz/225g plain wholemeal flour

4oz/100g plain flour

½ sachet easy-blend yeast

2oz/50g cut mixed peel

1oz/25g currants

1oz/25g walnuts, finely chopped

1oz/25g demerara sugar

2 tablespoonfuls sunflower oil

½ teaspoon ground cardamom

approx. 7 fl.oz/200ml soya milk, warmed

extra soya milk

Put the two flours, yeast and cardamom in a bowl and mix. Add the sunflower oil and combine well, then stir in the mixed peel, currants, walnuts and sugar and gradually add the soya milk until a soft dough forms. Knead the dough and return it to the bowl, cover and leave to rise for 1 hour in a warm place. Knead the dough again, then shape it into a ball and put this on a greased baking sheet. Flatten the ball slightly, cover and allow to rise in a warm place for 30 minutes. Brush the dough with soya milk, then bake in a preheated oven at 200°C/400°F/Gas mark 6 for 15-20 minutes until golden brown. Cool on a wire rack before cutting into slices.

St. Basil's bread

1lb/450g plain flour

½ sachet easy-blend yeast

½ teaspoon salt

2oz/50g vegan margarine, melted

1oz/25g demerara sugar

1 rounded tablespoon finely grated lemon peel

½ teaspoon ground cloves

½ teaspoon ground cinnamon

approx. 8 fl.oz/225ml soya milk, warmed

Combine the flour with the yeast, salt, sugar, cloves and cinnamon. Add the melted margarine and lemon peel, then gradually add the soya milk until a soft dough forms. Knead the dough well and return it to the bowl. Cover and put in a warm place for 1 hour to rise. Knead the dough again and shape it into a ball. Flatten this slightly and place it on a greased baking sheet. Cover and leave in a warm place for 30 minutes until risen, then cut a cross in the top of the dough. Bake in a preheated oven at 200°C/400°F/Gas mark 6 for about 20 minutes, until golden and hollow sounding when tapped underneath. Transfer to a wire rack and allow to cool.

DESSERTS

Greeks are very fond of their desserts, so much so that when they dine out they often finish their meal at one of the numerous pastry shops, where a wider choice of dessert is on offer. Filo pastry is undoubtedly the most versatile and is used in a variety of recipes. Cakes are also served, usually accompanied by strong Greek coffee. Fresh fruit salads are another popular choice and these are made with seasonally available produce such as melons, figs, oranges, apples, pears, peaches, grapes and apricots. Halva is a traditional Lenten sweet and there are many regional variations.

Fruited filo ring (serves 6)

10oz/300g filo pastry

2oz/50g vegan margarine, melted

sesame seeds

filling

8oz/225g eating apples, peeled, cored and finely chopped

8oz/225g dessert pears, peeled, cored and finely chopped

2oz/50g dried apricots, finely chopped

2oz/50g sultanas

2 fl.oz/50ml fresh orange juice

1oz/25g walnuts, finely chopped

¼ teaspoon ground cloves

Soak the apricots and sultanas in the orange juice for 1 hour, then mix in the remaining filling ingredients.

Place one sheet of filo on a flat surface, brush it with melted margarine and put the other sheets on top, brushing between each one with margarine. Scatter the filling evenly over the pastry sheets, leaving a 1 inch/2.5cm gap along the two longer edges. Starting at one of the long edges roll the pastry up to completely enclose the filling. Squeeze the roll to compress it slightly and make the pastry look crinkly, then carefully form it into a circle and transfer to a greased baking sheet. Brush with melted margarine and sprinkle with sesame seeds. Bake in a preheated oven at 180°C/350°F/Gas mark 4 for about 25 minutes until golden brown. Serve warm topped with yoghurt.

Baked nectarines (serves 4)

4 firm nectarines

1½oz/40g ground almonds

1½oz/40g sultanas, finely chopped

½oz/15g demerara sugar

2 tablespoons fresh orange juice

1 tablespoon orange flower water

Put the almonds, sultanas, sugar, orange juice and flower water in a small bowl and mix well. Cover and chill for 2 hours. Cut the nectarines in half and carefully remove the stones. Fill the hollow of each nectarine half with some of the almond mixture, shaping it neatly into a raised mound. Arrange the filled nectarines in a baking dish and bake in a preheated oven at 180°C/350°F/Gas mark 4 for about 25 minutes until just tender. Serve at room temperature, topped with yoghurt.

Fruity semolina pudding (serves 4)

2oz/50g semolina

1½oz/40g raisins, chopped

1oz/25g demerara sugar

1 rounded dessertspoon vegan margarine

1 teaspoon vanilla essence

18 fl.oz/550ml soya milk

ground cinnamon

Melt the margarine in a large pan, remove from the heat and stir in the semolina, raisins, sugar, vanilla essence and soya milk. Whisk thoroughly until no lumps remain. Return to the heat, bring to the boil while stirring and continue stirring for a minute or two until the mixture thickens. Divide between 4 serving glasses, cover and chill until set. Sprinkle ground cinnamon on top before serving.

Fig and orange salad (serves 4)

8oz/225g dried figs, chopped

2 oranges

5 fl.oz/150ml fresh orange juice

2 tablespoons white wine

¼ teaspoon ground cinnamon

6 cloves

1 dessertspoon orange flower water

Peel the oranges and keep a little of the peel for garnish. Remove the pith, membranes and pips, then chop the segments and strain the juice into a saucepan. Put the chopped segments in the fridge. Add the figs to the pan together with the 5 fl.oz/150ml orange juice, wine, cinnamon, cloves and flower water. Stir well and bring to the boil. Cover and simmer gently, stirring occasionally, until the liquid has been absorbed. Transfer to a covered container and refrigerate until cold. Mix the chopped orange with the cold figs and spoon into 4 glass dishes. Finely grate the piece of peel and use to garnish the desserts.

Baklava (serves 6)

10oz/300g filo pastry

2oz/50g vegan margarine, melted

filling

6oz/175g mixed nuts, grated

2oz/50g breadcrumbs

1 teaspoon ground cinnamon

syrup

2oz/50g demerara sugar

8 fl.oz/225ml water

1 tablespoon lemon juice

1 dessertspoon rose flower water

Cut the filo sheets in half to make 12 sheets of about 10 x 9 inches/25 x 23cm. Put 3 sheets on top of each other on a greased baking sheet, brushing between them with melted margarine. Mix the nuts with the breadcrumbs and cinnamon and sprinkle a third of the mixture evenly over the pastry, leaving a 1 inch/2.5cm gap around the edges for tucking in. Repeat these pastry and filling layers twice and finish with the remaining filo sheets. Brush the top with melted margarine and tuck the edges of the pastry under to enclose the filling. Cut through into diamond shapes, then bake in a preheated oven at 180°C/350°F/Gas mark 4 for about 25 minutes until golden.

Put the ingredients for the syrup in a small pan and stir well. Bring to the boil and simmer for about 10 minutes, stirring frequently, until the mixture becomes syrupy. Pour the hot syrup evenly over the pastry, making sure it goes down between the diamond shapes. Leave to soak in for about an hour before serving.

Rice pudding (serves 4)

6oz/175g long grain rice

15 fl.oz/450ml water

15 fl.oz/450ml soya milk

1½oz/40g demerara sugar

1 teaspoon vanilla essence

ground cinnamon

Bring the rice and water to the boil, cover and simmer until the liquid has been absorbed. Stir in the sugar, soya milk and vanilla essence and bring back to the boil. Simmer uncovered, stirring regularly until the liquid has been absorbed and the mixture is thick. Spoon into bowls and serve warm, sprinkled with ground cinnamon.

Dried fruit salad (serves 4)

12oz/350g mixed dried fruits (e.g. apricots, dates, apples, pears, peaches, figs, sultanas), chopped

14 fl.oz/400ml water

1 tablespoon rose flower water

2 inch/5cm cinnamon stick

6 cloves

Put all the ingredients in a pan and bring to the boil. Cover and simmer for 5 minutes. Transfer to a lidded container and keep in the fridge until cold. Remove the cinnamon stick and cloves and divide the fruit between 4 serving dishes. Serve topped with yoghurt.

Almond and apricot pastries (makes 6)

pastry

4oz/100g plain flour

1 teaspoon baking powder

1 tablespoon olive oil

approx. 2 tablespoons fresh orange juice

orange flower water

sesame seeds

filling

2oz/50g ground almonds

2oz/50g dried apricots, finely chopped

2oz/50g sultanas, chopped

4 tablespoons fresh orange juice

1 teaspoon orange flower water

¼ teaspoon ground cinnamon

Put the filling ingredients in a bowl and stir well. Cover and leave for 30 minutes.

Sift the flour and baking powder into a mixing bowl and stir in the olive oil, then gradually add the orange juice until a soft dough forms. Knead the dough well and divide it into 6 equal pieces. Roll each piece out on a floured board into a 4 inch/10cm square. Stir the filling again, then divide it between the pastry squares, placing it in the centre. Brush the pastry edges with water and fold the corners of each square towards the middle to form an envelope shape. Squeeze the pastry edges together to join, enclosing the filling, and make a couple of slits in the top of each pastry with a sharp knife. Brush the tops with orange flower water and sprinkle with sesame seeds. Bake in a preheated oven at 180°C/350°F/Gas mark 4 for about 10 minutes until golden brown. Serve warm with custard.

Orange-glazed peach slices (serves 4)

4 firm peaches
4 fl.oz/125ml fresh orange juice
½oz/15g demerara sugar
1 tablespoon orange flower water

Bring the orange juice, flower water and sugar to the boil in a large pan and simmer for 5 minutes, stirring occasionally. Remove the stones from the peaches and cut each peach into 8 slices. Add the slices to the pan and simmer gently, stirring occasionally, until they are just tender. Remove the peach slices with a slotted spoon and put them in a serving bowl. Boil the remaining liquid hard until it reduces, then spoon it over the peaches. Cover and refrigerate until cold.

Fruit and nut halva (serves 6)

4oz/100g semolina
4oz/100g raisins, finely chopped
3oz/75g vegan margarine
3oz/75g demerara sugar
2oz/50g walnuts, finely chopped
8 fl.oz/225ml fresh orange juice
1 tablespoon orange flower water
¼ teaspoon ground cloves

Put the sugar and orange flower water and juice in a pan and stir well. Bring to the boil and simmer uncovered, stirring frequently, for 3 minutes. Melt the margarine in another saucepan, add the semolina and move it around for 1 minute. Stir in the raisins, walnuts, ground cloves and the orange syrup and cook over a low heat, while stirring, for a few minutes until the mixture is thick and comes away from the sides of the pan. Spoon it into a wetted 7 inch/18cm square baking tin and press down evenly with the back of a spoon.

Cover and refrigerate for a few hours until cold and set. Run a sharp knife around the edges to loosen, then carefully turn out onto a plate. Cut the halva into small squares or diamond shapes to serve.

Pistachio and raisin fingers (makes 12)

10oz/300g filo pastry

2oz/50g vegan margarine, melted

chopped pistachio nuts

filling

4oz/100g pistachios, grated

4oz/100g breadcrumbs

2oz/50g raisins

4 tablespoons fresh orange juice

½ teaspoon ground cinnamon

½oz/15g demerara sugar

syrup

1oz/25g demerara sugar

4 fl.oz/125ml water

1 dessertspoon rose flower water

Mix the filling ingredients together. Cut the filo pastry into 24 pieces of about 9 x 5 inches/23 x 13cm. Lay 12 sheets out on a flat surface and brush them with melted margarine, then put another sheet of filo on top of each one. Divide the filling evenly between the pastry oblongs, placing it at one end only. Fold the two long sides of pastry over the edges of the filling, then roll each oblong up to completely enclose the filling. Arrange the rolls in a greased baking dish and brush with melted margarine. Bake in a preheated oven at 180°C/350°F/Gas mark 4 for about 25 minutes until golden.

Put the sugar, water and rose water in a small pan, bring to the boil and simmer for about 10 minutes, stirring occasionally, until the mixture becomes syrupy. Spoon the hot syrup over the hot fingers and scatter some chopped pistachio nuts on top. Allow to cool before serving.

Apricot and orange custard (serves 4)

4oz/100g dried apricots, finely chopped

6 fl.oz/175ml fresh orange juice

1 tablespoon orange flower water

14 fl.oz/400ml soya milk

1oz/25g cornflour

1oz/25g demerara sugar

toasted flaked almonds

Bring the apricots, orange juice and flower water to the boil in a small pan, cover and simmer for 15 minutes. Dissolve the cornflour in the soya milk and put in a blender with the sugar and the apricots and any remaining juice. Blend until smooth, then pour into a double boiler and bring to the boil while stirring. Continue stirring for a minute or two until the custard thickens. Pour into 4 serving glasses. Sprinkle the tops with flaked almonds and serve warm or cold.

Cherry lattice tart (serves 4)

pastry

6oz/175g plain flour

1 teaspoon baking powder

4 tablespoons sunflower oil

cold water

filling

1¼lb/550g cherries, stoned and halved

1¼oz/40g demerara sugar

1 dessertspoon cornflour

Put the cherries and sugar in a saucepan and cook uncovered, stirring occasionally, for about 20 minutes until the cherries are soft and the mixture is thick. Remove from the heat and stir in the cornflour.

Sift the flour and baking powder into a bowl and add the sunflower oil. Mix thoroughly, then add enough cold water to bind. Turn out onto a floured board and knead. Roll out two-thirds of the pastry to line a greased 7 inch/18cm loose-bottomed flan tin. Prick the base and bake blind in a preheated oven at 180°C/350°F/Gas mark 4 for 5 minutes. Roll the remaining pastry out thinly and cut it into ½ inch/1cm wide strips. Spoon the cherry mixture evenly into the pastry flan case and arrange the pastry strips on the top in a lattice pattern. Return to the oven for about 25 minutes until browned. Serve warm topped with yoghurt.

BAKING

The most important religious festival in the Greek Orthodox calendar is Easter and special cakes, biscuits and breads are baked at this time in celebration. Other recipes are popular throughout the year and meals are often rounded off with thick Greek coffee and a selection of cakes and biscuits. Walnuts and almonds feature strongly in many recipes and cakes are often flavoured with fresh orange and lemon juice. All the cakes and biscuits featured here are suitable for freezing.

Walnut and almond crescents (makes approx. 28)

3oz/75g walnuts, finely grated

3oz/75g ground almonds

2oz/50g breadcrumbs

1oz/25g vegan margarine

1oz/25g demerara sugar

pinch of grated nutmeg

2 tablespoons orange flower water

approx. 2 tablespoons water

Cream the margarine with the sugar, add the walnuts, almonds, breadcrumbs, nutmeg and orange flower water and mix thoroughly. Gradually add enough water for the mixture to bind together. Take heaped teaspoonfuls of the dough and shape them into flattened crescents. Put these on a greased baking sheet and bake them in a preheated oven at 180°C/350°F/Gas mark 4 for 12-15 minutes until golden brown. Carefully transfer to a wire rack to cool.

Sesame cookies (makes approx. 16)

4oz/100g plain flour

1oz/25g vegan margarine

1oz/25g demerara sugar

1 rounded tablespoon light tahini

2 tablespoons water

1 teaspoon baking powder

½oz/15g sesame seeds

Cream the margarine with the sugar and tahini in a mixing bowl. Work in the sifted flour and baking powder, then add the water and mix until everything binds together. Take heaped teaspoonfuls of the mixture and with damp hand roll them into balls. Roll these in the sesame seeds until completely coated, then shape them into 3 inch/8cm sausages and bend these into 'S' shapes. Flatten them slightly and put them on a greased baking sheet. Bake in a preheated oven at 180°C/350°F/Gas mark 4 for about 15 minutes until browned. Slide onto a wire rack and allow to cool before serving.

Easter biscuits (makes approx. 12)

6oz/175g plain flour

1½oz/40g demerara sugar

1oz/25g walnuts, grated

2 fl.oz/50ml sunflower oil

1 teaspoon baking powder

1 teaspoon vanilla essence

3 tablespoons soya milk

Mix the sugar with the oil and vanilla essence in a large bowl. Stir in the walnuts, then add the sifted flour and baking powder and finally the soya milk. Mix thoroughly until a soft dough forms. Take rounded dessertspoonfuls of the dough, roll into balls, flatten these and put them on a greased baking sheet. Bake in a preheated oven at 180°C/350°F/Gas mark 4 for about 15 minutes until golden. Transfer to a wire rack and allow to cool.

Almond cakes (makes approx. 16)

3oz/75g ground almonds

2oz/50g plain flour

2oz/50g vegan margarine

1oz/25g demerara sugar

½ teaspoon baking powder

1 tablespoon cognac

rose flower water

Cream the margarine with the sugar, work in the ground almonds, then add the sifted flour and baking powder and cognac and mix together well. Take heaped teaspoonfuls of the mixture and roll into balls. Flatten each ball slightly and place on a greased baking sheet. Press with a fork on top of each one and bake the cakes in a preheated oven at 180°C/350°F/Gas mark 4 for about 10 minutes until golden brown. Sprinkle the cakes lightly with rose flower water, then carefully put them on a wire rack to cool.

Semolina and lemon slices (makes 8)

4oz/100g semolina

4oz/100g plain flour

2oz/50g demerara sugar

4 fl.oz/125ml sunflower oil

4 fl.oz/125ml soya milk

juice and finely grated peel of 1 lemon

1 dessertspoon baking powder

  topping

juice of 1 lemon

½oz/15g demerara sugar

Combine the sunflower oil, sugar, juice and grated lemon peel in a mixing bowl. Stir in the semolina, then add the sifted flour and baking powder alternately with the soya milk and mix thoroughly. Spoon the mixture into a lined and greased 7 inch/18cm square baking tin and level the top. Bake in a preheated oven at 180°C/350°F/Gas mark 4 for about 30 minutes until browned.

Bring the lemon juice and sugar for the topping to the boil in a small saucepan. Simmer, stirring frequently, for 4-5 minutes until the liquid reduces down. Spoon the syrup over the hot cake in the tin and leave for 10 minutes before turning it out onto a wire rack. Cut into 8 slices once cooled.

Yoghurt and almond cake

8 fl.oz/225ml plain soya yoghurt

4oz/100g plain flour

2oz/50g ground almonds

2oz/50g vegan margarine

2oz/50g demerara sugar

1 dessertspoon baking powder

topping

½oz/15g demerara sugar

1 teaspoon almond essence

2 tablespoons water

¼oz/7g flaked almonds, chopped and toasted

Cream the margarine with the sugar, then stir in the ground almonds and yoghurt. Add the sifted flour and baking powder and mix well. Spoon the mixture into a lined and greased 7 inch/18cm round baking tin. Level the top and bake in a preheated oven at 180°C/350°F/Gas mark 4 for about 30 minutes until golden.

Put the sugar for the topping in a small saucepan with the almond essence and water. Bring to the boil and simmer briskly, stirring frequently, for 4-5 minutes until it reduces down. Brush the mixture over the warm cake and sprinkle the chopped almonds on top. Carefully transfer to a wire rack and allow to cool before cutting into wedges.

Raisin and cognac cake

12oz/350g plain flour

4oz/100g raisins, chopped

3oz/75g demerara sugar

4 fl.oz/125ml sunflower oil

5 fl.oz/150ml fresh orange juice

1oz/25g walnuts, chopped

finely grated peel and juice of 1 lemon

1 dessertspoon baking powder

1 teaspoon ground cinnamon

½ teaspoon ground cloves

3 tablespoons cognac

Combine the raisins, juice and peel from the lemon, sugar, cinnamon and cloves in a large bowl. Cover and leave for 2 hours. Stir in the sunflower oil, orange juice and walnuts, add the sifted flour and baking powder and mix thoroughly until well combined. Spoon the mixture into a lined and greased 8 inch/20cm diameter cake tin and level the top. Cover with foil and bake in a preheated oven at 180°C/350°F/Gas mark 4 for 30 minutes, then remove the foil and bake for 20-25 minutes more until golden brown. Make a few holes in the top with a skewer and drizzle the cognac evenly over the cake. Leave in the tin for 20 minutes, then transfer to a wire rack to cool completely. Serve cut into slices.

Spiced walnut cake

6oz/175g plain flour

2oz/50g walnuts, grated

2oz/50g vegan margarine

1½oz/40g demerara sugar

6 fl.oz/175ml soya milk

1 teaspoon baking powder

½ teaspoon aniseed, crushed

½ teaspoon ground cinnamon

¼ teaspoon ground cloves

½ oz/15g walnuts, finely chopped

topping

½ oz/15g demerara sugar

¼ teaspoon ground cinnamon

2 fl.oz/50ml water

Gently heat the margarine and sugar in a saucepan until melted. Remove from the heat and stir in the grated walnuts, aniseed, cinnamon and cloves. Add the sifted flour and baking powder alternately with the soya milk. Mix very well, then spoon the mixture into a lined and greased 7 inch/18cm round baking tin. Spread it out evenly and sprinkle the chopped walnuts on top, pressing them in lightly with the back of a spoon. Cover with foil and bake in a preheated oven at 180°C/350°F/Gas mark 4 for 25 minutes. Remove the foil and bake for another 10 minutes until golden.

Put the ingredients for the topping in a small pan and stir well. Bring to the boil and simmer for a few minutes while stirring, until the mixture thickens. Brush the syrup over the top of the cake, then carefully transfer it to a wire rack to cool before cutting it into wedges.

Lenten cake

6oz/175g plain flour

6oz/175g plain wholemeal flour

3oz/75g demerara sugar

2oz/50g cut mixed peel

2oz/50g currants

1oz/25g walnuts, chopped

4 fl.oz/125ml olive oil

7 fl.oz/200ml fresh orange juice

2 tablespoons cognac

1 tablespoon lemon juice

1 teaspoon ground cinnamon

1 dessertspoon baking powder

topping

1 dessertspoon demerara sugar

½ teaspoon ground cinnamon

Stir the orange juice, cognac, lemon juice, cinnamon, mixed peel and currants together in a bowl, cover and leave to soak for 1 hour. Whisk the olive oil with the sugar in another bowl, add the sifted flours and baking powder, the walnuts and the soaked fruit and soaking liquid and mix thoroughly. Spoon the mixture into a lined and greased 8 inch/20cm diameter baking tin and level the top. Mix the topping ingredients together and sprinkle evenly over the top. Cover with foil and bake in a preheated oven at 180°C/350°F/Gas mark 4 for 50 minutes. Remove the foil and bake for another 10 minutes or so, until the cake is browned and a skewer comes out clean when inserted in the centre. Carefully turn the cake out onto a wire rack and allow to cool.

Fruit-topped orange and aniseed cake

4oz/100g plain flour

2oz/50g semolina

2oz/50g demerara sugar

3 fl.oz/75ml sunflower oil

finely grated peel and juice of 1 orange

1 dessertspoon baking powder

1 rounded teaspoon aniseed, crushed

soya milk

topping

2oz/50g raisins

2oz/50g sultanas

2 tablespoons cognac

2 tablespoons fresh orange juice

1 tablespoon orange flower water

Finely chop the raisins and sultanas and put them in a lidded container with the remaining topping ingredients. Stir well, cover and refrigerate overnight, then transfer to a small saucepan and simmer for a few minutes until all the liquid has been absorbed and the fruit is soft.

Mix the sunflower oil with the sugar in a mixing bowl. Pour the orange juice into a measuring jug and make it up to 6 fl.oz/175ml with soya milk, then add it to the bowl together with the grated peel, aniseed and semolina. Mix well, add the sifted flour and baking powder and whisk the mixture thoroughly for a few minutes until it is thick and smooth. Spoon the mixture into a lined and greased 7 inch/18cm round cake tin, cover the top loosely with foil and bake in a preheated oven at 180°C/350°F/Gas mark 4 for 30 minutes. Remove the foil and bake for a further 10-15 minutes until golden brown and firm. Invert the cake onto a wire rack and carefully remove the lining. Spoon the fruit mixture evenly over the inverted cake and leave to cool before cutting.